To
Mayme Chinn
with
Best Wishes!
Ethel M. Jones

MY TWIN AND I

ACKNOWLEGMENTS

I wish to thank my sorority sister, Florence Wallace, who patiently deciphered my handwriting and typed all my copy, not just once but twice, and very often three or four times on certain parts.

She herself made the Xerox copies and helped assemble the pages, getting them packaged and ready for mailing. Besides that she has given me encouragement.

Ethel M. Jones

A week after her death I received a book from Eugenia Price, *Getting through the Night*, in which she quotes a verse from the Bible: "Weeping may endure for a night, but joy cometh in the morning," Psalm 30:5b.

At first I didn't see how that could be, but now I really feel joy, a strange, mystical kind of joy that I cannot explain. I feel that my sister is with me and I feel an urgency to write. That is the reason I am writing this.

I make no apology for trying to write a book that will lack the most wonderful things of all—romance and marriage. However, since it wasn't God's plan for us, I will try to show that single people can have joyful, fulfilling lives too, with some happy, exciting events.

Briefly, we had the usual childhood experiences, but, being twins, we had more mix-ups, too. Of course we had our "ups" and "downs" but mostly "ups," for which we were doubly thankful. In our periods of anxiety we were together and could help one another, thus dividing the worry. Since our mother's home was in California we had rewarding chances to travel and to attend the summer sessions at the University of California. After we retired from teaching we immediately became actively engaged in hospital volunteer work. Even after we came to this retirement facility we kept busy, joining a creative writing group and buying lapidary equipment, so that we could polish those rocks that we had found years before.

FOREWORD

In a slide program that my sister and I once gave on our hobby, rock collecting, Elsie quoted the last two lines from one of her favorite poems, "Collector" by Gene Moore:
"Enclosed in song these treasures lie
Locked in my memory chest."
Now, I have so many precious memories of our journey through life together for over eighty-one years that it is difficult for me to decide which ones to pull out for this book.
Again let me give one of Elsie's favorite quotations, that she used to put on her board at school:
"The journey of a thousand miles begins
with a single step."
I won't try to cover "a thousand miles" but shall try to mention the high points and show how we both increased in knowledge and in spiritual feeling, where I can say with Oliver Wendell Holmes in "The Chambered Nautilus":

"Build thee more stately mansions, O my soul!...
Till thou at length art free,
Leaving thine outgrown shell by life's
unresting seal!"

One time when our mother was in the hospital, we gave her a book, *Climbing the Heights*. That is what I'll try to show—that each step took us higher, with Elsie leading the way right to the end. When she was in the hospital three weeks before her death, she sang "Blessed Assurance" to me every morning as I entered the room. Her night nurse had taught her the words, and she sang in a good clear voice with much joy. I was amazed since I had never before heard her sing so well. Because she had faith, I believe she was able to go so peacefully.

CONTENTS

DEDICATION

This book is dedicated to my dear twin sister, Elsie Mabel Jones, who passed away on January 2, 1986. Writing this has been a dream of mine ever since 1981, when I had a story with this title published in *The Villager,* our monthly newsleaflet in Carolina Village. I even talked about it with Elsie, but it just remained a dream with me, until I found her notes recently. She had consulted her diaries and had jotted down chapter headings for what she considered the highlights of our life.

MY TWIN AND I

by

Ethel M. Jones

Illustrations by the Author

A Hearthstone Book

Carlton Press, Inc.   New York, N.Y.

PART I
EARLY LIFE THROUGH COLLEGE YEARS

A Hard Decision

"Shall we try to save your wife or the second baby?" That was the direct question put to our father by the doctors attending Mother on the day of our birth, March 26, 1904, in Jefferson, Ohio. In great anguish Father said, "Oh, try to save both, but if we have to decide, I suppose the little girl already here will need a mother."

I shall always be grateful to those doctors who saved Mother and after another half hour my twin sister. When I think of it, I can't find words enough to express how thankful I am that they succeeded and that I was privileged to live eighty-one years with my dear sister, who was my constant companion.

Pronounced Dead

Again our parents were in distress when a year later the doctor pronounced my sister dead and went home to get his wife to come and console Mother. In the meantime Father rushed to the kitchen and fried some onions, put them in a flannel cloth and put it on Elsie's back and chest. In a few minutes she was breathing again. When the doctor came back with his wife he was surprised. Later the trouble was diagnosed as polio. I had it too but not so severely. I must pay tribute to Mother also, for she massaged Elsie's left leg every day for a year or more, because she dragged it for a long time.

Family Tidbits

Our father was much older than our mother; in fact, old enough to be her father. He was living when the Drake oil well was drilled in Titusville, Pennsylvania, in 1859. His imagination was fired by that discovery and he spent a lifetime in the oil business. He was born in Slippery Rock, near Pittsburgh, but left home at an early age to seek his fortune. He never found the fortune but he did find Mother.

She liked to tell it. She was attending a teachers' meeting in St. John, New Brunswick, Canada, where she taught school. He entered the room with a friend and saw her. Immediately he asked the friend, "Who is that beautiful girl over there with the black curly hair? Can you get me an introduction?" He did, and later they were married. He proudly brought her back to the States to Titusville and then, Ohio, where we were born.

Father was a strong man, weighing about 200 pounds, and was over 6 feet tall. One time when we were living in West Virginia, and he was in his seventies, he picked Mother up in his arms and carried her upstairs after she had had surgery because the ambulance attendants couldn't negotiate the sharp turn in our stairway with their stretcher.

He was strong in his convictions too. He was against alcohol and gambling, and people knew it. In fact, he sometimes embarrassed us. If we were on a street car, and a man started to swear, Father would get up, tap him on the shoulder and say, "There are ladies present."

He guarded us with a vengeance. One time we were on one of those open street cars with a a running board all along the sides, when the brakes failed and the car started fast down a steep hill. Without hesitation he grabbed me and jumped, landing on the dirt roadway.

He was ahead of his time in many ways. We ate whole wheat bread, only fresh garden vegetables, and good tested meat. We drank no coffee. I remember him, carrying a big live turkey under his arm to bring it home (to be sure it was fresh).

When he married Mother he was working for an oil company, studying every geology book available, going over the territory

BRAKE FAILURE
on TROLLEY

and taking leases. I am proud that he was able to discover good locations and make money for his company, so that now when I read about some of these big companies giving grants to colleges, etc. I say to myself, "My father had a little part in that." He even went to see John D. Rockefeller at one time, but I don't know what it was about or when!

I can't leave "Family Tidbits" without telling a little something about Mother. No matter how much I wrote, it still would not be adequate to describe her good qualities and her devotion to her family. Mother was born in St. John, New Brunswick. Her grandfather, a Methodist minister, had come from London to Prince Edward Island, where her father, Thomas Durdan, was born. After he grew up, our grandfather went to New Brunswick, where he married Bessie Graham. They lived in St. John until Mother was married. Later her parents moved to California.

Because they had a very strict religious background, when Christmas happened to come on a Sunday, Mother and her two little sisters sat and looked at their dolls under the tree but waited till Monday to play with them. Mother wanted to be a nurse, but her father wanted her to be a teacher and sent her to Normal School in Frederickton. She could have gone to McGill but did not have the money. She liked to tell us that the principal of Queen's High School came to her house one night to tell Grandfather, "That girl of yours made a 100 on that math test for entrance to McGill."

She taught only four and a half years before she got married and then came to this country. Our father was so proud he would not let anyone "take care of his family;" so she never taught school again. She did have a chance, however, to teach us (and be a nurse too). I remember when we started in high school and came home in tears that first day. We just couldn't understand that algebra. How could you add two figures to find the difference? Mother got the thermometer down off the wall and had us count a certain number of degrees above zero and so many degrees below, and then we counted the degrees between the top figure and the bottom one. It was clear and we were happy.

Mother liked poetry and was able to quote whole poems. "The "Spider and the Fly" was one she often recited for us, even when she was in the hospital for the last time. We didn't care too much for the doleful ones like "The Beheading of Anne Boleyn." She liked "The Lady of the Lake" and often quoted from it. My sister and I too liked to teach that poem. Another favorite was Whittier's "Snow-Bound." She especially liked the digression on "death" where only the author and his brother were still alive. When I had finished reading it to her one day, she said, "Read it again." That makes me recall when we were small and she read "Peter Rabbit" to us; we both chorused out, "Read it again!" just as she finished it.

When we were little and we dropped a dish and broke it, Mother would ask, "Who did it?"

We both said, "She did it," and pointed to the other.

Giving up, Mother then would say, "Well, whoever did it, don't do it again."

Double Troubles

Most mothers may have only one child at a time getting into mischief, but Mother always had two. One day when we were about two years old, she took us to a neighbor's house to visit. While Mrs. Seger and Mother were visiting in the living room, Elsie and I went exploring into another room. We found a jar of musterole and we knew what that salve was for. We wanted to play doctor, and there, right in front of us, was a cat. What good luck! One of us held the nice friendly cat while the other applied the grease over it liberally. When we decided it was cured we let it go, and it went meowing into the living room. I know Mrs. Seger must have been dismayed when she saw her pet. I don't remember. Mother brought us both home, and I presume Mrs. Seger set to work degreasing her cat.

Gypsies

One day when we were still living in Jefferson. We were playing in our big front yard when we saw a band of gypsies coming down the street. Immediately we ran to our large pine tree and dived in under the thick branches that came down to the ground. We kept watch until the gypsies got out of sight.

Mrs. Seger's Cat

Then we ventured out and ran up to the house.

Mother was so happy to see us. She had been worried because she had seen the gypsies too and couldn't find us. She had gone to the back door and the front door and looked out all the windows, but there was no sign of us. It seems we had hidden from her as well as from the gypsies.

More Childhood Experiences

We both liked animals very much, although our father had warned us about strange dogs. One day Mother was walking down the street with us and I spied a dog up ahead. I ran up to it and put my two hands around its mouth so it wouldn't bite me. Mother had to come to the rescue, while Elsie just watched. That must have been a most friendly dog!

Inexplainable Things

There were many things that we could not explain. Why was it that when one of us got hurt the other felt the pain too? When we were babies, Mother kept a pink ribbon around my wrist, and a little later Elsie wore a gold chain with a little heart on it around her neck. (That was the only way we could identify ourselves in a picture.) Mother was confident she couldn't get us mixed up, but she was puzzled sometimes by the turn of events.

Why was it that when one of us fell and broke her collar bone, the other one went around with her hand on her shoulder saying, "It hurts?" Why was it that one time when she was bathing us and spilled some hot water on my foot, a red blister appeared on Elsie's foot in the same position as the one on mine?

In school we often had to change our answers on our homework, because, when we compared them, we had the same original sentences to show the meaning of our spelling words. We did not want our teacher to think we had copied each other's sentences; so we took turns in changing them.

In 1910 when we were six, we moved from Ohio to Clarksburg, West Virginia, and lived there until 1922, when we graduated from Washington Irving High School. Besides the usual round of school experiences, a few events stand out in our memory. One was learning to play the piano, which we enjoyed very much. We would have continued with the lessons but our music teacher left to do war work in Washington, D.C. We had learned enough so that we could go on ourselves playing new pieces, especially the wartime songs like "Over There" and "Till We Meet Again." A close friend and her little sister came to sing with us.

During the war we did our little part by planting "Victory" gardens. I had a little crop of peanuts from a plant I had sent off for. Most exciting of all was the Armistice Day celebration. The firetrucks came through the streets at 5:00 A.M. and woke us up with their sirens going. We hurriedly dressed and joined the crowds thronging the streets, all headed for the newspaper office where news was flashed on a screen.

Speaking of newspapers, I was editor of our school paper in the eighth grade but I can't remember what we put in it. Anyway I have a picture showing me with the staff. I guess I must have liked to write, for I won a prize for an essay contest in high school and had to go up on the stage (a real ordeal) to get it. The subject was "What America Means to Me." The prize was $5.00 but it looked like $500.00 to me. I proudly opened a bank account with it.

When we had the junior-senior prom in the gym, there were booths for various features, and in one, matching book titles with the names of students my sister and I were put down beside *Innocents Abroad*. We helped with the yearbook, but didn't have anything to do with the jingles beside the pictures. Somebody had written beside mine, "What can I do to be forever known?" Now the prophecy, "Latin teacher," turned out to be right.

Before we graduated, the oil company managed by Father was sold and he took his share of the money and invested it in drilling more wells and they all came in "dry holes." Although he was past retirement age, the president of his former company took him on again and told him, "Send those girls to college." There weren't any scholarships in those days, and we were thankful that Father got on a salary list—no more "wildcatting" with the chance of losing everything.

Even though times were hard we went on a motor trip through Virginia in 1918, and in 1920 we went by train to Erie where Father's sister-in-law lived and then on to Niagara Falls. Our father loved to show us things and explain geological terms—like synclines and anticlines as we looked out the train window. He made up jingles to entertain us. For example:

> "Here we go
> On the B & O
> And it beats the
> dickens
> For going slow."

While he managed the little independent oil company we lived a leisurely life. We went to our summer home in season. Father even built a bridge with benches along the sides over the run near the river. He made a garden and tapped a sugar maple in season and made maple sugar for us. We went picking berries and gathering nuts—in short—just an idyllic sort of life—independent and carefree (for us at least).

Father's Daughters

My sister and I both took after our father in looks and disposition. Mother was very quiet, unassuming, and patient. Father was outspoken and ready to talk with anyone. He wrote letters to state governors or congressmen to express his views. I have done so occasionally but have felt like doing it more often.

Father wrote letters to Mother every day that he was away from home and wrote to us before we could read. Mother kept our letters tied up in a little bundle. The gist of his message was, as I recall, "Now be good little girls and obey your dear Mama."

He wanted to write a book about the early days in the oil country. He was cheated many times, but I doubt if he would have put that in a book; nevertheless, he was happy. Mother told us about one time when she had invited a young oil worker to the house for dinner. The phone rang and this man heard Father say that he would take the first train in the morning to procure that lease he had been trying for ten years to get. The elderly lady who owned the land kept changing her mind, but this time she was ready to sign. The visitor got up from the table, making some excuse, caught the midnight train, hurried to the woman's house and got the lease by pretending that our father had sent him. Consequently, he received the reward offered by the company—one-eighth interest in the well, and that made him a millionaire. (Father never got anything except his salary.)

Too Vivid a Description

Shortly after we moved to Clarskburg, Mother took us to a neighborhood Sunday School. One day we both came home scared and crying, to tell Mother that a man came into our class and told us all about that fiery region below us. His description must have been too vivid, for we were afraid and did not want to go there. Father happened to be home that day. He got up, put on his hat and asked Mother, "Where does this man live?" The next Sunday Mother took us to another church uptown. I hope we weren't "cry babies."

Little Angels

At Alta Vista school (Even our school had a Latin name.) the teachers had a hard time telling us apart; so they just called a name and expected the right twin to answer. If they had observed us writing, they could tell, because Elsie was left-handed; but the trick was to remember which one wrote with her left hand. I don't know if we poked one another to answer or not. We could have easily enough, for we sat together at one desk, since we had just one set of books.

Our geography book was so big we could hide behind it (or thought we could). One day in the third grade we were called on to give the state capitals. We knew them, for we had studied at home and while the teacher was busy with the other side of the room, we had time to play, giggle, or watch the others from behind that big book. After we spieled off those capitals, the teacher said, "Now, you see, those girls have been studying." We were happy, but we weren't any "little angels."

Childhood Pleasures

The "horse and buggy" days weren't over before our time. With what delight my sister and I greeted the news that we were taking a surrey and horses (rented from the livery stable) to drive out into the country for the day! Although this mode of travel was slow and had its inconveniences, still for us as children those problems were nonexistent.

What fun it was, when a sudden shower came, to help our parents hurriedly fasten the curtains up! I don't know if Mother thought it was fun. How cozy it seemed inside! We didn't have a care. Even if we got stuck in the mud, we knew Father could get us out. There weren't any roadside picnic tables, but the food tasted just as good while we sat on the ground in some farmer's field. One time when it rained we made ourselves at home in a vacant, deserted farmhouse. We even played that it was haunted.

As to our diversions, we got along with an occasional movie and a few comic strips. (They were really comic too, not hair-raising dramatic nightmares.)

School days were happy days. We could take flowers to our teacher without being called a "brown-noser" or whatever the slang term for it is at the present time. We enjoyed working and playing with all our classmates, not just a few in a clique. We didn't have "dates" in the seventh grade. Every weekday evening we sat around the dining room table doing our lessons. There was nothing else to do.

In our reading we liked *The Five Little Peppers and How They Grew*. In literature class we studied the well-known classics, full of wonder and excitement, like *Treasure Island*. We were not expected to be interested in things beyond our experience. At our tender age we did not worry about bombs and problems of peace. We were not trying to carry the weight of the world's troubles on our shoulders like some giant Hercules.

Little pleasures delighted us, like getting a free ice cream soda, when we bought our books at a certain store on the first day of school. All through life simple things pleased us, and it was fortunate that they did, for we had neither time nor money for expensive pleasures.

Elocution Lessons

All the time we were in high school my sister and I took osteopathic treatments for our curvatures. The doctor's office was just a block below where I went every Saturday morning to take elocution lessons while Elsie was taking her treatment.

Mother thought I needed help in overcoming my timidity, so she paid money for me to learn how to stand, breathe, and exercise my vocal cords like a singer. I never was a singer and neither did I become an orator. I do remember memorizing selections to show the different qualities of my voice. Some of the lines I recall to this day: "Roll on, thou deep and dark blue Ocean, roll!" to show the orotund. "Darius Green and His Flying Machine" was useful in showing the aspirate (whisper): "Hush," Reuben said, "He's up in the shed," and the nasal, "The birds can fly and why can't I?" The most use I got out of this poem was saying it for my Latin class when we studied Ovid's story (simplified) about Daedalus and Icarus.

After we were settled in our new home on Buckhannon Avenue in Clarksburg, we became acquainted with our neighbors. Jean Post and her sister Helen were our closest playmates and our lifelong friends. They visited us in Morgantown and in Charleston the first year we were there. They stayed in the governor's mansion because the governor was their uncle. Mother was in the hospital at the time and Father had come home. When our friends came to our house, Father went to the kitchen to look for something to treat them to. Because we weren't cooking much with Mother away, he couldn't find anything but some thin sliced dried beef that he himself had just brought from Pittsburgh. He brought in a plate of dried beef and crackers to pass around, and we were surprised and somewhat embarrassed.

Jean still lives in the red brick house where she was born and we recall the days watching the squirrels in the big cage in their yard. Her father had the first car in the neighborhood and we went with them every evening "to the farm" ten miles away to milk the cows.

The second person to own a car near us was a doctor, the father of one of our friends. One day he left the car in the drive, and the daughter got in it, started it but didn't know how to turn it off. Therefore we (Elsie and I were with her) drove around and around our block until the gasoline was gone. Then we got out.

One time after Jean and Helen had been playing the piano and singing war songs with us, we had a light snack of buttered crackers Mother had prepared. Their little brother had come with them that evening, and when there was only one cracker left on the plate, he looked at it and finally asked, "Jean, is that your cracker?" Mother heard and passed it to him, but Jean was embarrassed. Don't tell me "children can't think."

Days at W.V.U.

It's hard to condense four years of college life into a few pages. Since our father traveled most of the time, it made no difference where our home was. We moved to Morgantown, West Virginia, where we made new friends, and Mother had new neighbors. Ours was the last house of five new ones built on a street called Mansion Avenue. (There wasn't a mansion on it.) Mother said that Father always managed to choose the last house on the last street in town. We did get plenty of exercise going to the post office for our mail and going down to the campus for our classes.

Mother had a small garden planted "by the moon" and was pleased when her plants grew luxuriously, surpassing those of our neighbors, professors in the College of Agriculture.

Needless to say, we had the usual round of parties, entertainments, clubs, and football games. We even sat out in the rain sometimes to watch a game. We enjoyed the Press Club because we were taking journalism in our sophomore year, and were working on *The Athenaeum,* our weekly paper that was newspaper size.

Our "run" included interviewing professors and reporting speeches and other programs held in Convocation Hall. Since we knew no shorthand, we used Latin words in our notes instead of English ones if they were shorter (like *se* for 'themselves'). Between us we could get most of the speeches. The

23

busier we were the happier we were. Here are two lines from a poem' "A Reporter's Life" we wrote:

"On we struggle day and night
To bring the campus news to light."

Besides graduation itself, our greatest thrill came from being elected to Phi Beta Kappa. In fact, it went to my head to such an extent that I thought I had to have a store-bought dress for the dinner and reception. Elsie was more sensible, for she wore the pink dress that Mother had made. Fourteen of our professors that we had had were Phi Beta Kappa and were there. If you had seen them on the campus carrying their green book bags you would also have known that most of them were Harvard men.

Languages had always fascinated us. Therefore we were really interested when our Latin professor had written on the board one day a passage that we were to translate in French, Spanish and Italian, as well as the Latin, so that he could point out the similarities and roots.

After we had started teaching we took a year of German in night school given by a professor from a nearby college. Another year we took Italian from the American consul in Charleston. We enjoyed these classes because they were so small and informal.

Also since we were not taking them for credit, we did not worry about grades. When the professor of German asked us to go to the board to conjugate some verbs, all six of us took our places and compared what we had written with what our classmates on either side of us had.

Elsie and I did a little extra practicing on the way home. As we got near our house, I asked her if she had the key, *"Has du deinen Hausschlussel mit?"* She would answer, *"Ja."*

I remember one idea that I gained from an epistle by Horace entitled *Ara Poetica* that we read in Latin class at W.V.U. Horace, in giving advice to would-be writers, suggested that after you have written something put it away for a few years, then get it out, read it again, and if you are satisfied, have it published.

I waited twenty years before I let anyone see my little article, *"The Mystery."* I wrote it down early one morning in 1948, after pondering all night over the mystery of the universe.

What disturbed me was an article I had just read that day in a magazine that seemed to indicate that everything was a matter of chance.

I used part of my little essay in a church circle meeting, where I said:

"Let the scientist study the problem of the origin of the universe and let the philosophers speculate as to its meaning. As for me, just let me enjoy the miracles of nature without worrying about mysteries that are too big for me to comprehend. To me, the aimless wandering of particles of dust does not explain the formation of a universe any more than a chance collection of a few daubs of paint on a canvas, without an artist's guiding hand, can explain a beautiful picture."

I concluded with a thought from a prayer: "Make me grateful for what is clear and leave the rest for faith and love to disclose."

Twins in Class

When we were sophomores in West Virginia University we had a little Latin class of six members, and five of us were twins. One twin had lost her sister. The others were seniors then, so we did not have them with us in our senior year.

We were saddened that year because our professor was suffering from terminal cancer and not able to be in class the last month. My sister and I, having had eight years of Latin, were given the responsibility of taking over the large class of premed and prelaw boys, but they did not take advantage of the situation (which was to their credit) out of respect for our professor, who was ill.

Another time we got a little unexpected experience in teaching was in our sophomore year. We were taking journalism and worked on the *Athenaeum,* our paper. The professor had one freshman English class, and somehow it fell to us to grade all their themes. Perhaps he thought it would give us valuable experience. We took a big stack of papers home each week. (They didn't have paid readers in those days.) We rather enjoyed doing it, although we were loaded down with work ourselves. We went to great pains to keep this task a secret, but somehow it got out.

One day after we had moved to Charleston, had retired and were doing volunteer work, we met a prominent doctor in the hall of the hospital. Out of a clear sky he said, "Thank you for passing me in Freshman English."

Joining a Church

Ours was not a sudden conversion that led us into the church, just a gradual realization that something was missing. We had gone to Sunday School and church through the years. Mother put us on the Cradle Roll in a church near us in Jefferson, but Father said, "Wait until they really know what they are doing before joining."

We studied books like *Manhood of the Master* and *Faiths of Mankind,* but still didn't feel any desire to join until we were in college. The student director of the M.E. Church in Morgantown was very friendly and a good teacher of our Bible class.

As luck would have it, the minister of that church, Dr. Lowther, joined our little Latin class one semester, and we got acquainted with him. In fact, he generally walked part way home with us every day at noon because we passed the parsonage on our way.

Elsie and I had talked about joining a church, and our Latin professor brought out the differences between the Christian faith and the pagan beliefs that we were reading about in studying Latin authors. One day Elsie and I both spoke up at once on our way home from class and said to Dr. Lowther, "We would like to join your church!"

He probably was surprised, but he said, "I'm delighted! I'll come up to your house to see you and your mother."

When we got home, we told Mother and she started to dust the furniture in the living room, before we got lunch on the table. She was happy too, and when Dr. Lowther came, he asked if we had been baptized. Mother explained to him that our father wanted to wait until it would mean something to us.

The next Sunday we went to Sunday School as usual, and then in the church we sat on the front row with Mother. She took care of our hats when we went forward. Naturally we had to be bareheaded and had to kneel to be baptized. We really felt inspired and happy. After the service Mother and we were surrounded with people commenting on the "beautiful service."

Geology Classes

We could not leave our account of the years at W.V.U. without mentioning our two courses in geology, especially since our father studied geology all his life. In the first course, we enjoyed going on field trips taking our little hammers, not knowing that someday we would be "rockhounds." One time we even walked ten miles!

The course in historical geology really inspired us. After we had studied about the geological timetable and memorized those eras and periods, our professor made it clear that such a wonderful organization of everything in the universe had to have an organizer behind it. We knew he meant a divine organizer.

Our father saw no conflict between evolution in science and a belief in God. In later years we heard a Baptist minister say that the discoveries the astronauts were making served to illuminate God, not to eliminate Him.

Joy Personified

This chapter was written on June 22, 1986, just after Vesper services in Carolina Village where I am now living. The Chorale sang some joyful hymns, and our chaplain, Dr. Earl Brendall, gave a wonderful talk on "Joy in Religion." Immediately I thought of Eugenia Price, because she is always full of joy, and this was her birthday. Pictures of her on the jackets of her books show joy. You can see it in the big bright eyes and the smile on her lips—just the way she looked as a child, when I had her in the eighth and ninth grade in Lincoln Junior High School in Charleston, West Virginia.

I had seen Eugenia for the first time the previous summer (1926) on the very day that our moving van was unloading our furniture. She was with a group of children playing in the yard a across the street and singing "Happy Birthday" to our new neighbor's little girl (Clara Alice Thomas) on her tenth birthday.

Later, of course, I was delighted to see Eugenia coming into my class. I remember telling her father, our dentist, while he was using that grinding implement on my teeth (between strokes of the drill): "Eugenia is just...a little ball...of sunshine...coming...coming...bouncing...into my classroom."

I did not think of the word "sunbeam" then, but today I do, because Dr. Brendall in his talk on "Joy" referred to the joyful singing led by the early evangelists of the day. He mentioned the song children used to sing—"Jesus wants me for a Sunbeam" ending with "I'll be a Sunbeam for Him!" That stirred up vivid memories with me, for I remember being in a big chorus of school children and singing that at one of the evangelistic meetings.

It had not occurred to me at any time in all those intervening years that perhaps we should continue "being a sunbeam for Him" or, at least, a light to help others to the joy to be found in being a follower of Jesus.

Dr. Brendal touched on that too when he was talking about the joy in singing—"making a joyful noise unto the Lord." He reminded us that we should be like children and quoted, " A little child shall lead them." He also stated that we could remember the words of a hymn better than any prose writing because we sing it.

This week when we are thinking about freedom in our land, as we prepare for the celebration of the restoration of the Statue of Liberty, I am reading again Eugenia Price's book, *The Wider Place.* In a broader sense it is always appropriate to talk about the freedom we have in God's "wider place."

Coming back to the children, I used to keep a quotation on my board at school. For the first day I always chose this one by Henry Van Dyke:

"Let every morning seem to say;
'There's something happy on the way.
God sends love to you.'"

I meant it for the youngsters, but one day it dawned on me that it was meant for me too—that He was sending love to me in letting these darling little children come rushing into my room. Eugenia Price was one of them.

E.S.P.

Did we have "extra sensory perception?" All through our lives we always thought of the same thing at the same time. Often in a conversation we both spoke up in unison, and someone would say, "Now wait a minute! I can't listen to two at once."

One day after we had started teaching in Charleston, West Virginia, I came home from a shopping trip with Mother and said to Elsie, "Guess whom I saw today?"

Without hesitation she answered, "Helen De Berry!"

I was surprised. How could she know? Miss De Berry was our Latin teacher in high school in Clarksburg, and we had not seen her for several years. What made Elsie think of her? It is still a mystery.

California Here We Come

"California Here We Come!" That's what our hearts were singing as we started out for California in 1928. At last our childhood dream was being realized. Our father had entertained us when we were very young by describing just how some day we would get on a train and go to see Mother's father on the West Coast.

The sad part about it was that Father was not going. He went as far as Cincinnati with us and then got on an L & N train to go south to Tennessee where he was working. We headed west to St. Louis and Kansas City on our way to Los Angeles.

In the station in St. Louis we became acquainted with a teacher on her way to Seattle, where she lived; we noted that she was Phi Beta Kappa and she said she had gone to the University of California. That's where we hoped to go some day, and indeed we did. Four years later, would you believe it, we met her again in International House in Berkeley, where we all were staying. That was serendipity—meeting a good friend by chance.

In Kansas City the station was all decorated with flags, banners, and posters. The Republican National Committee was meeting there for their convention that election year and it was crowded. We almost got left behind. When we were asked to show our tickets coming through the gate that night, we didn't have any. They were back in our Pullman. The trainmen just knew we were "green" and let us through.

The Santa Fe train we were on made scheduled stops at towns along the way at meal time to let us eat in the Fred Harvey restaurant in the station. That gave us a welcome chance to exercise and also to get better acquainted with our fellow passengers. I remember one Englishman, who had evidently been watching us, asked, "Do you keep diaries?"

When we answered affirmatively, he remarked, "I thought you were the type." Now what did he mean by that?

We were so glad that we took the side trip to the Grand Canyon, for that is certainly a natural wonder we would not want to miss. In fact, we probably had our mouths agape in awe half the time, exclaiming over everything we saw.

As soon as we arrived in Los Angeles, we took a street car to Long Beach to get our first glimpse of the ocean. When we got off the car we fairly ran to the beach, as if it could get away from us. It was there for us to marvel at, and every time we went to the West Coast it was still there.

It is there yet, reminding me of an article in *Today's Health* that I once read. A dentist, Dr. F.C. Dickinson, in describing his trip through the Redwood Empire to the Pacific Ocean, marveled at the big trees, so much older than he. Later when he saw the ocean and realized that it was much older still, he felt he was almost as old as the trees. Then he looked up at the stars, the oldest of all, and felt that the redwoods and he were almost as old as the ocean. So he concluded that "time is timeless" and that we all belong to "some infinite scheme of life that will never end."

That made me think of Psalm 8, verses 3 and 4; "When I consider thy heavens, the work of thy fingers, the moon and the stars, which thou hast ordained, What is man, that thou art mindful of him?"

Naturally this first California trip was full of surprises and wonder for us. In San Francisco Aunt Juanita, who lived three hundred miles north in Arcata, Humboldt County, met us and piloted us around to see all the sights, such as the seals on Seal Rock near Cliff House.

We were amazed like everyone else, when we first saw the redwoods. We even drove through one tree and later sent a postcard view of it to our friends back home. We sent other cards, too, especially the one quoting the six stanzas of a poem by Joseph B. Strauss entitled "The Redwoods." He is also known as the builder of the Golden Gate Bridge, so that we have another reason to be grateful to him.

Indeed, when I stood in one of those beautiful redwood groves, I felt as if I were in a cathedral, with the tall trees like spires letting the sunlight shine through in slanting lines, as though they were stained glass windows. I recalled the last two lines of the poem by Strauss.

"Sink down, Oh, traveller, on your knees;
God stands before you in these trees."

Although our aunt had taken us to the beach several nights to see the moonlight on the water, it was the trip up the Oregon Coast that gave us the most inspiration. We had stopped at a motel in Brookings just across the highway from the beach. Mother, who was with us, had the bed near the front window, and we were at the back of the room."

Around midnight Elsie and I both woke up, and Elsie said, "It's moonlight!" We got up and quietly went to the big front window and looked at the moon making the waves and their whitecaps shine with brilliance. We recalled lines from Carruth's poem, "Each In His Own Tongue," and whispered low to each other:

"Into our hearts high yearnings
Come welling and surging in."

Before long Mother was half awake and asked, "What are you doing?"

"Looking at the moon on the waves," we chorused. She was used to the ocean, having lived on the East Coast till she was married.

"Yes, it is pretty, isn't it," she said and went back to sleep.

Delegates to P.T.A. Congress

In March 1929 my sister and I were both chosen to represent our schools at the National Congress of the P.T.A. in Washington, D.C. I had just been elected secretary of our group for the fourth year and that was my reward. My sister had taken care of publicity for her P.T.A. for four years.

We had a special bus, and that meant we had the use of it and driver the whole time we were there. We saw both the Senate and the House in Session, had tea at Senator Goff's house, went to the Smithsonian, and as a climax, shook hands with President Hoover and had a group picture taken on the lawn with President and Mrs. Hoover. We went through the White House and, of course, managed to attend a few meetings of the P.T.A. Congress. Mrs. Hoover spoke at one of them.

This reminds me of the time our circle at the church had a dinner meeting. One of the members had just returned from Washington, where she had attended the wedding of a relative to one of the Johnson girls. The minister came up to her saying, "Oh, let me shake the hand that shook the hand of the President!"

To come back to the bus trip, we had one bad time on the way home. After we had stayed all night at Natural Bridge we headed west on the Midland Trail (Old U.S. 60) the next morning but didn't get far. After some time the driver discovered the gasoline had been stolen. The rest of the trip we had an old, smaller bus that was sent to meet us. It was 2:00 A.M. when we got home (tired but happy).

Other Organizations and Activities

In our earlier years in Charleston we found time to attend the Open Forum, the A.A.U.W. meetings, and programs of all kinds. The most memorable concerts were given by the Navy Band, Sousa's Band, Madame Schumann-Heink, and Fritz Kreisler. An outstanding lecturer was Richard Haliburton. Also we were glad for the opportunity to hear E. Stanley Jones and Gypsy Smith.

Every year the Classical Section of W.V.E.A. had a luncheon meeting at the annual convention. In 1952, since I was chairman of that section, I attended a workshop in Buckhannon at Wesleyan College to prepare for the convention. It was so cold that summer in July that I went to nearby Elkins and brought a wool suit.

Mother and Elsie went along for the trip and enjoyed staying at the hotel and going next door to an old-fashioned store to browse around, where one could find everything from a harness for a horse to dishes from England. They bought dishes—big plates with scenes on them that we used on Thanksgiving and Christmas Day after that.

Even though it was work we enjoyed being on committees, like the legislative committee in the retired teachers' group, because it brought us together for a common cause. That group of retired teachers gave us something to look forward to each month, meeting former associates and having a social hour after the program. At the end of the year they always had a banquet, which was a pleasurable event in our social life.

We also had enjoyable dinner meetings once a month at Church Circle (business and professional group). There again we took our turn as officers. Preparing devotions was the most challenging duty.

At our church we had our turn serving on the Communion Committee of six, with two of us working up to be chairmen each year. The year we had charge we got along very well with help from the others. There was one worrisome time, however. We went to the church in plenty of time that Sunday, so we thought. When we opened the cabinets, we saw a light green powder on the outside of the velvet bags containing the silver; we started to wash everything. When the minister came in. Elsie told him our trouble and said we would be so glad when our third member came to help us.

"That's just what I came to tell you," he said. "She just called—can't come."

"Oh, me!" We hurried and managed to get everything done and in place before anyone entered the sanctuary.

Another time, when the communion was at night, we had left our car on the street near a parking lot. After we finished our work, the minister and his wife drove us around the block to our car. As soon as they had gone and we got started, a car waiting on the lot pulled off and got right behind us as I could see in the mirror. They stayed behind us till we crossed the river and then took a short cut so that they got ahead of us at an intersection. They went on down a deserted street that we usually drove on. They stopped and I waited for them to move on. Finally they did, crossing the railroad tracks and stopping in a wide place at the side of the street to wait.

By then I was making a sharp angle turn into a side street that came in at a "Y". Looking back we saw them backing and turning to come over the tracks toward us. I stepped on the gas, got to a built-up section with traffic lights, sped up a hill, and took a roundabout way home, thus eluding them, whoever they were. I couldn't tell if there was more than one in the car. It was too dark.

Mixups!

I will start with those mixups that occurred most recently. In November, 1984, when Elsie was being dismissed from the hospital after surgery, I was sitting in a wheelchair in the hall, and Elsie was still in her room with her special nurse.

Suddenly a nurse's aide started off with me and yelled over toward the desk, "I'm taking her down!" I told her I had a sorority sister who was coming to pick me up at the emergency room entrance. When we got there I said, "You can leave me here. I'll watch for her through this glass door."

"Oh!" she exclaimed, "It is absolutely against the rules of this hospital to leave a patient unattended!"

"But" I said, "I'm not the patient!"

With that, she turned and went back to the elevator.

In the meantime poor Elsie was in her room alone, deserted and wondering where everybody was. Her "special" had taken her bags, etc. downstairs. The friend who brought her station wagon to drive her home had taken the discharge papers to the office. My sorority sister got me home ten minutes earlier and brought me up to our apartment in my wheelchair, and then started down with the chair, so that Elsie could get in it. Unfortunately she got lost in our halls and went to the wrong entrance, and Elsie was left again sitting alone in the station wagon, while her friend came looking for the wheelchair. My two friends finally got together and Elsie arrived at our room where I was waiting for her.

Another Mixup!

One time in Charleston we both had appointments with the opthalmologist. Elsie was called in first, and the doctor kept saying as he was calling out numbers for his assistant to put on her chart: "Of course, you know, as you get older your eyes will change."

When he was through, Elsie said, "Ethel is coming in next."

"Ethel!" he exclaimed. "This is Ethel I have here."

"No," she said, "I'm Elsie."

Turning to the assistant, he said, "Now that whole chart will have to be copied."

All she could say was, "Well, how did that happen?"

Elsie was nearsighted and I have always been farsighted.

Another time when Mother was in the hospital for an extended stay, we thought it was a good time for me to have a mole near my lip taken off. The next day my sister was in the hall and the doctor who assisted my surgeon, met her and said, "I operated on you yesterday."

"No," she said, "I didn't have any operation."

He insisted, "I took a mole off your face."

She pointed to hers near her lip on the left and said, "It's still here!"

He looked bewildered, and then she told him she had a twin sister who had a mole removed from her face near the lip on the *right*, not the left. Going down the hall a little farther a patient called out from her room, "Your face looks much better today." So the doctor wasn't the only one who got us mixed up.

One evening when I was in the hospital. Elsie started for home and was near the elevator when another visitor saw her and went running back to the nurses' station, saying. "Your patient is getting away from you. She's at the elevator now."

The nurses probably knew what it was, but one of them came to my room anyway and found me in bed, much to their relief. We did have a little laugh over it.

Twin to the Rescue

Even though I had taken elocution lessons, as mentioned in a previous chapter, I still got stage fright. One day in a class in education at W.V.U. we were to give two-minute talks, and if we could not, we were to stand and wait for the two minutes to end.

My turn came and I stood by my chair. The professor had turned around, gazing out the window and was supposedly listening contemplatively to the speakers. I got through one minute of my talk, and in the middle of a sentence I hesitated from fright.

Elsie, sitting at my elbow, spoke right up, not only finishing my sentence but continuing to use the remaining time. The professor turned around, said, "Very good," and I sat down, greatly relieved that the other students did not give me away. The chairs were arranged like a U with the teacher's desk at one end, so that we were facing one another. They did manage to contain their mirth until we were cut in the hall. Years later one of the members of the class came to my building to teach, and the first thing she said, when she saw me, was, "Remember the time when your sister finished your speech!" Postlude: We sometimes wondered if that professor could detect any difference in our voices. Probably not. If one of us spoke and Mother was in another room, she often asked, "Who is speaking?"

Our Destiny

When we graduated from W.V.U., one of our professors said it was our duty to get married, and most of them wanted to separate us, but we had other ideas. Consequently we sent out applications ourselves, thereby taking the responsibility for the outcome. It was Oliver Goldsmith in *The Traveller* who said, "Our own felicity we make or find."

We did love children, all ages, and were delighted when we received word from Charleston that there were vacancies in the junior high schools there. We took pleasure in teaching other people's children (about 14,000 between us) and found the junior high youngsters so full of life and enthusiasm. They always came hurrying in the first day with someone asking, "How do you say this in Latin?" It wasn't long till they could say, I love you" (*Te amo*).

New Experiences in California

Besides being in California for the first time in 1928, we had many other new experiences that year. For example, we rode on a hand car on the railroad track and also in the engine of a logging train.

Mother's cousin, the son of the founder of the logging company, took us up for a day's excursion to a redwood logging camp in the high mountains, where we ate lunch at noon in their big dining hall. Then we watched the men at work in their logging operations.

Here comes the Crab!

To get there we sped along on a hand car over the high trestles, where the view was superb, but I was afraid to look down into those deep valleys below us. Coming back we rode with the engineer on a big high seat in his cab on the logging train. As a souvenir I still have the redwood burhl bookends my grandfather made for me from a block of wood I had seen lying on the ground. I asked what they were going to do with it, and they answered, "Just scrap," and gave it to me.

We also bought some redwood burl souvenirs in the Stump House in Eureka. The gift shop is inside a large tree stump and was always crowded with visitors.

Another new experience was going crabbing. I was always scared of crabs, but this day on the beach I threw my line out, and before long one of those big king crabs (the size of a dinner plate) was nibbling on my bait coming it toward me. I reeled the line in slowly, as my aunt had directed, so that the crab would not let loose of the bait. We also had to watch to see that we got enough bait on, so that it would last until he got near us, where we could reach him.

I was so excited I forgot I had on a long red coat and stepped into the water, but I stopped when someone yelled to me. Otherwise that coat might have been floating on the ocean. My grandfather came up with a gaff and net to dip the crab out of the surf. We had boiling water in a large washboiler on the beach near our camp, and in went the crab. Needless to say, we all enjoyed that crab for lunch. There was enough for the whole family.

The camp itself was new for us. The tent had an elevated wooden floor on which there were two double beds. My aunt was so afraid that we would get cold she even put a hot water bottle in under the piled-on blankets. We nearly roasted and threw them off at midnight.

Another new fishing experience was picking up fish with our hands. One morning early we were walking along the beach when our attention was attracted to a big flock of sea gulls squawking or cackling noisily as they dived down into the waves. We soon knew what it was all about, for a big wave left the fish wriggling on the sand right at our feet as the water receded.

I stooped down as fast as I could and got my hands full of

Elsie and Ethel's mother, a picture of delicate beauty.

Father Jones cuts a dashing figure.

Ethel (left) and Elsie (right).Even as children, they were inseparable.

Can you tell Ethel from Elsie? Hint: Ethel is on the right.

Four sets of twins, circa 1928. Back row: Ethel Jones (left) and Elsie Jones (right). Middle row: (from left) Eleanor Hill, Jean and Jane Hester, and Eleanor's twin brother Earl. Front row: (from left) Margaret and Jackie Ackerman.

August, 1954. Ethel (left) Elsie (right) proudly display their rock collection.

February 1971. Elsie (left) and Ethel (right) as volunteers at Charleston General Hospital.

Ethel (left) and Elsie (right) in February, 1969, showing a few samples of rocks collected in the deserts and
beaches of northern California.

silvery fish, but had no place to put them, so I pulled off my red felt hat. In no time I had it full of surf fish. We returned to my aunt's cabin and she helped us discard those that touched the red felt and cleaned the others. We fried them for our lunch, an unexpected, delicious meal.

A little farther north along the coast we went salmon fishing from the beach. This time we just watched our grandfather bring them in. On the same trip we boarded one of the salmon fishing boats but had to be careful where we stepped as there were big fish lying everywhere on the deck.

The whaling station at Trinidad head was closed, but we did find some fishermen cutting up a huge whale at a station at Field's Landing south of Eureka. That was interesting, but we had to hold a cloth that had been saturated with some kind of deodorizer to our faces. It had been supplied by the attendants there. We were unprepared for such a need.

The best fun for us, however, was in looking for agates. When our aunt asked, "How would you like to go to the beach today to hunt for agates?" We did not know what agates were.

Since we were always ready to go to the beach, Elsie said, "Yes," and I reiterated her answer. Our aunt knew the best places to hunt, so we bundled up. (It's cold in northern California along the coast.) The beach at Patrick's Point, where we went, is really dangerous, for there is a heavy undertow. (They say there is a fifty-foot drop off a short distance out from shore.) The beaches are all marked "No Swimming." It's a good thing I was not on that beach when my coat touched the water as I was crabbing. There is a steep trail down to the beach and a log across a little run to serve as a bridge. We always carried something for a cane and even held on to branches overhanging our path.

We were delighted with the agates that we found, and I had beginner's luck in picking up three large pieces of petrified wood that I had polished later. We also found jasper, a few pieces of jade, and fossils, and the sand dollars were so numerous we only picked up one.

Usually we stood at the water's edge, watching for the waves to roll the agates in. If the sun was shining they were easier to see, being translucent. Sometimes we sat on the dry sand and raked across the pebbles with our hands to look for one in our little "hole." Later we bought a trowel.

We were reminded of lines from Gray's "Elegy:"
"Full many a gem of purest ray serene
The dark, unfathomed caves of ocean bear."
This trip started a lifelong hobby for us.

When we came home we just brought the "special" things we found, as baggage space was limited. We did enjoy showing them to our friends and sharing them. At night we could close our eyes and see sparkling "jewels" on wet sand with the sun shining on them. That made us think of Wordworth's poem, "Daffodils," where he said:
"They flash upon that inward eye,
Which is the bliss of solitude."
We liked to give some of our "jewels" to our homeroom pupils and see their amazement when they held the translucent agate up to the light. Then we recalled Sara Teasdale's poem, "Life Has Loveliness to Sell" (or "Barter"). The two lines we liked best were:
"And children's faces looking up,
Holding wonder like a cup."
When we went to the desert, we were reminded of Gray's "Elegy" again:
"Many a flower is born to blush unseen
And waste its sweetness on the desert air."
After we had traveled and seen all these wonderful things, the poems we had studied in our high school and college days meant so much more to us.

More Twins

We came home from our 1928 trip to California, feeling richer in that we had more relatives than we had realized. Among them were three sets of twins. Mother had three first cousins, and all three of them had twins, so there were four sets of twins at one time in Arcata, where our aunt lived.

We had a picture taken on the lawn where the little Hill brother and his sister lived. Also in the group were the two little Hester girls. They lived in Oakland. The Ackerman twins, a boy and a girl, lived in Hawaii, and they shared our birthday, for they were born on March 26 also. We were the oldest, being twenty-four at that time. We had another picture taken of the twins and their mothers.

Intellectuals Abroad

On our first trip to Berkeley, California, when we went to see the head of the Latin Department at U.C., he was not in. However, we were surprised when we saw the janitor wearing a Phi Beta Kappa key and pushing a big broom. He came up to us and began talking in Latin. Afterward we learned that he spoke Latin, Greek, and Hebrew. He had been so disappointed that he had just missed being a Rhodes Scholar that he had stayed there to be near his beloved Classics Department. .

Then we were startled again when we got on a street car, and the conductor was wearing a Phi Beta Kappa key. We began to wonder what kind of competition we would have out there. Probably the conductor was just on a summer job, but I don't know about the janitor. He was there two years later when we went back. This gave us something to write home about.

Speaking of Rhodes scholars reminds me that here is a good place for me to say a word about out alma mater, West Virginia University. In a recent alumni magazine I noted that the University had had twenty students named Rhodes scholars (not a bad record for a university the size of W.V.U.). The same year, 1985, was the first time that a woman graduate was so honored at our university.

Talk about competition, we had it at U.C., especially in the two Latin courses we took in 1929 under Dr. A.T. Walker, from the University of Kansas. There were twenty in each class, mostly junior college and high School teachers from cities across the nation. We worked hard but enjoyed it.

In fact, one night Elsie woke me up at 3:00 A.M., because I was still sitting up in bed with my glasses on and "Cicero's Letters" in my lap, but I had been sound asleep. That's when I needed that invention that I saw pictured and advertised once that would let you learn while you slept. It was called a cerebrograph, and I was going to write a "story" about it, but never saw it advertised again.

Not all our time was spent on work during those forty-three years in teaching. Although it was work for Elsie, writing letters to Dr. Oscar Voorhees, secretary of United Chapters of Phi Beta Kappa, to request information about forming an Association inasmuch as there were over forty members living in our area. The results were rewarding.

Elsie's principal, F. Ray Power, was a member and had asked her to do this. He was pleased when she received a reply in a few days and a copy of a model constitution. The next year, after we had contacted other members, we formed an association for the purpose of promoting scholarship. To that end we soon were able to provide some scholarships to local high school students.

We met in an assembly room in the public library once a month in the evening. We had speakers and discussions on various timely topics. After the meetings Elsie and I walked to our bus stop a few blocks away. One of the members escorted us to our bus stop.

We didn't know he was a widower living in a big home down the street until after he had passed away. He was brilliant and witty, serving as our president for four years. We noted too that he left several millions to various charities. Someone said, "You didn't play it right." No, we were happy and content and completely disregarded our professors' advice, when they wanted to separate us after graduation.

In March 1929, we had a luncheon in honor of Dr. Voorhees. In December near the anniversary date of the founding of the Society (December 5, 1776) we held a banquet and every succeeding year thereafter. There were usually fifty to sixty members present, and the meals were served in style at a hotel. From 1932 to 1935 I was secretary-treasurer, and the only trouble was that I had to sit at the speaker's table. Yes, those were big occasions for us, whom our classmates at W.V.U. had dubbed "shrinking violets." By 1935 the membership of the association had climbed to 84. They were not all teachers by any means. We often had the governor, members of the legislature, judges, and lawyers, as well as officials from the big Carbide and DuPont plants.

Under social events we might include a few from our days at the University of California. In 1929 and 1930 we stayed at a fraternity house (Kappa Alpha Theta) near the campus. Miss Lent, a home economics instructor at U.C., had charge of two houses during the summers—ours and the Phi Mu house across the street with sixty girls as residents.

One group of girls entertained those in the other house once a week alternately. Upon Miss Lent's advice we consulted a doctor, who gave us shots regularly for anemia and told us to drink a quart of milk a day. That's where the girls got their idea for a cartoon ("Guess Who") about us. It was easy to guess, because there were two girls in the picture, each with a glass of milk and wearing a big ØBK key.

On the first day of class one time, Elsie and I sat on the front row as usual. Another student asked, "Are you Phi Beta Kappa?" We were surprised and said, "Yes."

Then she explained that the front row was reserved for "Phi Betas." Not knowing their traditions we had innocently been advertising our membership. Then she sat down beside us and we presumed she was a member too and asked her. She was. We often wondered if she had thought that we were "in the wrong pew."

A Health Crisis

In the summer of 1930 we were carrying a heavy schedule including Latin (Elegiac, Poets), Celtic literature, and bibliography making. We both went to see a woman doctor, who was not only an osteopath but a surgeon and medical doctor as well. Elsie needed treatment for her curvature. This doctor checked me, went out to her kitchen telling me to lie still. Soon she came in with a big plate loaded with toast and mashed-up liver all over it. "Your blood is as low as it can get and you still live," she said. "Now both of you go to this little ice cream parlor on the corner and get sundaes every time you come here (twice a week)." So we did. That wasn't hard to do. I still remember those good pineapple sundaes.

Anyway, we managed to keep going and on the last day for classes just after our final exams, I landed in the hospital in Berkeley with a bad attack of something. Since we had been in a room for some time and no one had come around (after the first nurse got me in bed), I said to Elsie, "Get me out of here. That ferry leaves in 15 minutes and then we have to board another ferry to Sausalito; if we miss that, we miss our train to Eureka."

So she helped me dress. We just walked out. If any people saw us, they probably thought we were visitors. We hailed a taxi and told the driver we had to get to the Oakland ferry building in a hurry. We had a wild race through the streets and just made it. I don't see how my sister managed, holding on to me, her purse, and a suit case. Going through the gate to the boat, a sailor fell against me and said, "'Cuse me, it's hard to keep an even keel." I hope no one thought I was in the same condition.

After we boarded our train, the conductor wanted to call ahead to get an ambulance to meet us at some stop in the woods (all redwood country now). I insisted on going on as I wanted to get to Mother.

When we did arrive in Eureka my two aunts were with Mother, and before long I was in the St. Joseph Hospital. That evening I remember turning over enough to look out the window overlooking Humboldt Bay, and the sky was all aglow with a glorious sunset. I thought this night might be my last; I hope I said a little prayer. I woke up thinking it was morning, but it was midnight and the operation for appendicitis was all over. The doctor said, "You must be carrying a horseshoe in your pocket." I know now it wasn't just luck.

Before closing this chapter let me add that I really thought I was going, because I had heard the nurses talking in the hall and their voices came through the open transom. "She is going to die," they said, "She is a teacher and came clear across the continent to be with her mother." Some time later I found out that the patient across the hall had died from a ruptured appendix, and they were talking about her.

Our Future Home

In 1931 we visited Hendersonville, North Carolina, the site of our future home, but we did not know it then. Father was working in Tennessee trying to discover a source of natural gas for Knoxville. To make a long story short he did locate a well that came in two million cubic feet a day and he was elated.

That was the time he raised his own salary in a most unorthodox way simply by putting down a larger figure on his account going into the office. He was so happy he said, "Let's celebrate; we'll take a trip through the South."

We came through Gatlinburg and to the state line where the road ended; so we went back to Marshall, and then up to Asheville. It was June (just time for the Rhododendron Festival) and we stayed there a week.

Father thoroughly enjoyed the parades and festivities, and so did we. Then we visited Hendersonville and all the surrounding area.

In 1980 my sister and I moved to Hendersonville because Carolina Village offered just what we needed after retirement. We were happy to be in a place Father liked. He did enjoy the cool air and beautiful scenery.

That fall Father had a fatal heart attack and we were glad we had stayed with him during the summer. He had walked sixteen miles in the country just the week before to locate a well.

He liked to tell about the fast L & N train stopping for him out in the "middle of nowhere." Passengers started grumbling, "What's wrong? Why are we stopping here?" He grabbed his bag and the conductor let him off just a few yards from the location of the well. Of course, his taxi man managed to get his car over the field later that day to pick him up, and he made plans for a road to be built to the well. I hope it came in a good "producer."

The American Dream

Just recently, on August 5 to be exact, a large headline in a newspaper caught my eye. It said, "American Dream Found in Lottery's Winners." Is that the American dream we read about in history? For us it meant the ability to work and earn a living, perhaps making enough to save for one's old age. It also meant freedom to choose what is best for oneself, an opportunity to learn and develop one's best qualities.

Our father did not make a fortune. His good friend from the early days did, but the friend lost his only son in World

War I, and his wife died in her fifties. He lived in a mansion surrounded by servants until he was ninety. I hope he was happy, but we felt sorry for him.

On the other hand, when our father died he had Mother and the two of us with him. The bank had just closed, and he said, "Well, girls, I'm not leaving you any money."

We replied, "You provided us a happy home and the opportunity to get an education, so that we can make our way."

Now you can decide for yourself which one was the happier man.

As far as we were concerned, our "American Dream" came true, and I am grateful.

Note: Since writing this I saw the results of a study made by Colonial Penn that shows among older people the most precious possessions are children, friends and relatives, not material things.

A Torn Shirt

As usual in those early days of teaching, I felt I was being initiated, having to run a three-ring circus in the morning homeroom period. Between bells we had ten minutes to take the roll, collect "banking" money, write excuses, and sell tickets to whatever games we had that day. This day was no exception.

I was seated at my desk selling football tickets, and the pupils were in a single line coming up with their money. Suddenly out of the corner of my eye, I caught a glimpse of someone running behind me. I reached out quickly with my right hand to catch him, but I only got hold of his shirt: riipp! I heard it and thought, "Oh, dear, now what do I do?"

Fortunately I kept the top drawer of my desk full of stuff, just for emergencies. I had a big needle already threaded and scissors; so I said, "Hold still till I sew your shirt!" He was quiet and didn't say a word. Maybe he was wondering what his mother would say.

The pupils in their seats were quiet too, but every so often someone would say. "Stick him, Miss Jones." When I finished, ready to let him go, and had cut the thread, I noticed that in my hurry I had sewed his shirt to his undershirt. Then I had to do it all over, and he was subdued. I worried and hoped I wouldn't hear from his home. I didn't.

Is it any wonder then that I came up short $5.00 at the end of the day another time, when I had sold game tickets in the morning? After looking everywhere, even in my purse, wondering if I had enough money to replace the five, I thought about the wastebasket placed near the door at the back of my room. I spread some newspapers on the floor and dumped that basket. Was I glad to see that "greenback" come rolling out among the discarded papers!

Depression Years

After Father's death in 1931, we needed to take Mother away for a change. We put our goods in storage and bought tickets for California, in the summer of 1932, so that she could visit her father and two sisters in Humboldt County, while we were in summer school in Berkeley. We couldn't work on a degree in our field, since no Latin courses we needed were offered, but we did sign up for two courses, one on the junior high and one in psychology. Later we met Dr. Walker in the hall and he said if he had known we were coming he would have offered another course in Latin.

Naturally we wanted to see Dr. Deutsch, but he was now president of the university, so we did not make an appointment. Luckily we met him in the hall, and he was surprised that we had come out in a "depression year." He was pleased that I had translated a poem by Tibullus into English verse, and he said, "Not many continue to study after a course is over!" (We had had a course under him two years before.) I'll quote four lines from the poem, as it seems to me the subject matter is appropriate today, when we are striving for peace.

> "What madness it is to call black Death
> To us by waging war,
> It comes on silent feet in stealth
> And is ever hanging o'er."

This was not my only attempt at versification. While still in W.V.U. I had tried it with a few verses from Horace (Ode 4, Book I). It, too, is on a doleful subject. Here are four lines from it, translated from the Latin:

"With lamb or ewe appease his ire.
For lo! pale death prepares the pyre
And knocks with stern, impartial malice
At poor men's huts and royal palace."

Elsie did not translate Latin poetry into English verse, but she did enjoy writing in a lighter vein. One time when we had had a sudden, surprise snowstorm in May, she wrote fourteen stanzas about it. We were in our first year at West Virginia University, and she handed in her poem, "Winter's Return," for an English assignment.

Here are the fourth, sixth, and eleventh stanzas:

"The winds, let loose, roar through the town
And scatter objects up and down.
Away to shelves go summer gowns,
And out come coats of black and browns.

"The little birds no longer sing,
For cold it is upon the wing,
But vainly search for grains of food
With which to feed the hungry brood.

"By noon the snow had left the earth,
And Spring smiled forth in jolly mirth.
The honey bee began to hum
And stretch his legs no longer numb."

As you can see the storm was soon over, but it gave Elsie something to write about.

A Summer to Be Remembered

The best of all our trips to California was this one in 1932, when we lived at International House in Berkeley, while we attended the summer session. The I House, as it was called, was located high up on the hill near the stadium and overlooking San Francisco Bay. That experience was thrilling and invaluable to us, because it was different and full of the unexpected. The House, which was financed by the Rockefeller Foundation, was similar to the one in New York. When we applied we did not know whether we would be accepted because so many rooms had to be reserved for different nationalities.

When we arrived, a guide met us, explained the combination to our mailbox, and the buzzer system, gave us a handbook, and took us to our rooms. (Yes, two rooms. No double beds were allowed.) We were a little dismayed, for we had never slept apart from one another. After we went to bed that night, neither of us could sleep. Elsie tapped on the wall between us to let me know she was awake. Then I got up and went to her room, as I carried her key and she had mine. I crawled in with her, talked a few minutes, and fell asleep. When I awoke she went back with me to let me in my room for the rest of the night. We had a great time peeking out our doors to see if the hall was clear. After that we stayed where we belonged. I guess the single room, with one desk, etc. was more conducive to study.

One outstanding event each week was the Sunday night supper, when we not only met students from all over the world but heard outstanding lecturers talking on world affairs. We sang songs in different languages while the notes and words were flashed on a screen. A native led us, using a pointer to touch each word.

Another advantage to living at I House was being able to go on the tours planned for us. For example, we went with a group to Chinatown and ate in a Chinese restaurant. We learned to eat with chopsticks and our Chinese guide told us many interesting things.

The tour that my sister and I enjoyed most was on board a Japanese liner. That was different. We had eaten many times before in a Chinese restaurant, but taking our shoes off and sitting on the floor on deck the Tatsuta Maru was different. The sukiyaki was delicious, prepared right there in front of us.

When I was going with the crowd on a tour of the five decks on this luxurious ship and shaking hands with the captain, I never thought that in a few short years we would be at war with Japan or that a little later (in 1948) I would be corresponding with a Japanese journalist, managing editor of Radiopress, who wanted to know something about American schools. He had seen an article of mine in *The Nation's Schools* in the library in Tokyo. For twenty years I sent him my school paper, which I sponsored. He was greatly interested when he learned that I had been on that ship, Tatsuta Maru, for he had too. Sadly he told me it had been torpedoed, as had her two sister ships. He and his wife were Christians and sent me Christmas and Easter cards.

We hated to leave our friends at I House, when the term was over. It made us think of a poem Mother always quoted when we moved. It was Longfellow's "Ships that Pass in the Night." When summer school started, six weeks seemed like a long time to be with our friends. Now that it was over, it seemed like an instant, just long enough to say "Hello." The poem says, "So on the ocean of life we pass and speak one another."

Ambassadors of Good Will

As I recall those wonderful, carefree days at International House, the thing that impressed me most was the friendliness of the students of all nationalities. It reminds me of a poem written by a high school student in Detroit, Melvin Wachs, in 1947, and printed in the paper *Jambo* for the Boy Scouts going to the World Jamboree in France. In five beautiful stanzas he portrays the need for brotherhood. Alluding to the lack of knowledge of other languages, he says,

"And with youth's friendly eyes
Smiled what we could not say."

Every year after this, when we had a program to observe Brotherhood Week in our guidance class, someone always read this poem. There is a wealth of material on the subject, but this poem and a baccalaureate sermon by Rabbi Alfred G. Minda in Minneapolis were outstanding in their appeal and were appreciated by young people. In fact, each year when we had an oratorical contest, some one memorized the speech by Rabbi Minda. It was called "America the Beautiful" and stresses the line "Crown thy good with brotherhood."

If only the nations could do what the students at I House did, or the Scouts in their jamboree, perhaps we could attain world peace. My sister and I were privileged to be a little part of the program at Berkeley. Perhaps some day there will be more student exchanging, leading to a better understanding of others.

The Olympics

While living in International House we made many friends, who did so much for us. One of our best friends lived at Los Altos, close to Palo Alto. She invited us to her home the weekend that the United States Preliminaries for the Olympics were being held in Palo Alto. In watching the track events we felt the crowd of 60,000 was bigger than any we had ever been mixed up with before. We enjoyed meeting her family and picking figs from a tree (a new experience for us).

Besides watching the events on the field, we had a chance to see President Hoover's home. It gave us a thrill to see the beautiful mosaic at the entrance to the chapel at Stanford University. This side trip was really inspiring. We had visited the Stanford campus on our first trip to the West Coast, when I got cactus needles all over my suit. This time I kept watch.

As I said before, this was during Depression years and prices were very reasonable. At I House we could get a good breakfast for 30 cents (including ham, eggs, toast, cereal, coffee, and cream). In San Francisco one cafeteria offered a full lunch for 20 cents. Another bargain we took advantage of was the Sunday Pass. We paid 25 cents to get on a street car for the first ride and then kept getting transfers to go anywhere all day long with no extra fare.

Now, it's time to head for home. In Toledo we got on a "luxury train," the Sportsman, and discovered we were the only passengers all the way to Charleston. We didn't even wake up when we got there at 3:40 A.M., but when we woke up at 7:00 we found our car on a siding and a cab waiting for us, right beside the train. The driver got our check and then got our trunk for us. Everybody in those days of adversity was always trying to help someone else.

Postlude

In 1929 when we saw President and Mrs. Hoover in the White House, we did not know that we would see them again in October of 1932.

One Saturday morning, October 22nd to be exact, the President was scheduled to make a talk at 8:50 at Laidley Field in Charleston on his way to Detroit. This was the first time for us to be in a presidential crowd since the John W. Davis nomination ceremony in Clarksburg in 1924.

The Parkersburg Band was the official escort for the President's party, and a cannon fired a twenty-one-gun salute. Some Girl Scouts presented Mrs. Hoover with flowers. After the speech we went over toward the tracks, that run right along by the stadium, to watch President and Mrs. Hoover board their train and wave goodbye from the rear platform. The streets were so crowded it took us a long time to get back down town.

After we became "rockhounds" we read in a mineralogy book that Mr. and Mrs. Hoover in 1912 had translated Agricola's 1564 work, *De Re Metallica,* from the Latin, thereby making a great contribution to our literature on minerals and mining. Naturally we were interested too because Agricola wrote in Latin.

Combating Hurricane in Washington

On July 3, 1933, we had a letter from my aunt in California saying she and a friend were coming to the World's Fair in Chicago the first of August and would come to see us. That helped us to decide about buying a car. I had been taking driving lessons first to see if I could handle it before buying one.

We bought a Chevrolet with a trunk rack on the back, and on August 11th I got my license after failing once. The first time I didn't give any hand signals. I told the state policemen who took me for the test that I looked in the rearview mirror and because there was no one behind me there was no reason for signals. The day after I passed the test, I drove to the C & O station to meet my aunt and felt so proud. If she was scared to ride with me she didn't show it.

On August 20 we started for Washington, D.C. My aunt and her friend were postal workers and wanted to see the Capitol. I don't know if they went to see the Postmaster General or not. The first stop I made did scare my aunt, for I pulled off the road to a lookout place, where you could see the river gorge 500 feet below. She yelled, "Oh, my gosh!"

The next time I told my passengers what I was doing. In

New Market, Virginia, we stayed at a hotel, the only brick building in town, I think. We had nice connecting rooms, only $5.00 for all five of us (still Depression prices).

When we came to cities of any size I let May, Juanita's friend, do the driving. It was pouring rain when we reached Alexandria.

In Washington, we let May get on a one-way street, and she said, "Five pairs of eyes and no one saw that sign!" Other drivers were yelling at us all the way up the block. She did get turned around, and we took the first hotel we saw—right there on the corner.

The next two days we saw the usual places in our sightseeing, but the third day, when we came out of a big store, the taxi man said, "You had better get under cover; there is a hurricane on the way." So we went to our hotel, but May and Juanita, not being used to anything but earthquakes, decided to do more sightseeing.

We had just got in our room on the eighth floor, when the electric power went off, and the bellboy brought us candles. My aunt and her friend finally came in all out of breath from climbing eight flights of stairs. When we looked out the window, we saw cars moving down the street with no drivers. Over 1000 trees blew over, we found out later. The sirens and fire trucks were going all night. We passed the time playing rummy by candlelight.

Since the rain had ceased, we decided the next morning to try to get home. As luck would have it, the only two roads open were U.S. 50 and 211 going south, just the way we wanted to go. Washington had had seven inches of rain the day before, and we had to drive through water over the running boards. No, I wasn't driving. I let May do it, and she wasn't used to anything like this either in sunny California. The only casualty we had was a flat tire. We had picked up a nail in the flooded streets somewhere. The roads to Arlington and Mt. Vernon were blocked, so we had had to take an old road. Patrols were out putting red lanterns at the hazardous places and guiding us around fallen trees.

The attendant where we bought gasoline before crossing the Blue Ridge noticed our flat tire and put on the spare from the trunk rack. We enjoyed the trip down the beautiful Shenandoah

Valley. When we came to Lewisburg in our own state, we stayed at the General Lewis Hotel. (The Greenbriar at White Sulphur Springs was a little too expensive for us.)

The General Lewis was like a museum, and we looked at relics from Revolutionary days, like powder horns and hoop skirts. We had a trundle bed under our bed, which was so high you needed a step stool to get on it. Needless to say, we were very happy when we got home the next day.

Journalism Tour

In 1934 during the Christmas vacation we went on a journalism tour sponsored by Marshall College (now University) to New York City by train and boat. The day before we left, I remember going into a drugstore to buy something for seasickness as everybody told us to be prepared. We did as advised and I felt so silly asking for "Mother Sills Seasick Pills" that I could hardly get the words out for giggling. Elsie was just as bad, and I don't know what the clerk thought. Anyhow we got the pills but didn't have to take one.

Three of our best friends, who were also teachers, the Goodall sisters, went with us and stuck right with us through all our difficulties. We left Charleston at the unearthly hour of 3:15 A.M. and got to Norfolk at 1:30 P.M. When we saw our boat we were a little uneasy, because it was the Madison, the same boat that had been badly damaged in the Hurricane the year before. We were in that storm in Washington, you remember, and we had saved a picture of the damaged boat.

At breakfast the next morning two Charleston girls, Jean Guthrie and Mary Lee Settle, who were studying Journalism, sat at the table with us. They had both been pupils at Lincoln at one time. Mary Lee is now a noted writer.

As we neared New York we were thrilled to see the Statue of Liberty and the skyline of New York at sunset. It made me think of this, when I saw the Statue this year on the Fourth, thanks to T.V. There were sixty-five on this trip (thirty from Charleston). I suppose most of them had seen the Statue before, but for us it was the first time, and we were really inspired thinking of all that it symbolized.

We went to the Paramount Hotel, had dinner there, and

then went to Rockefeller Center and Chinatown. That was the end of our sightseeing, because Elsie got sick. We called the hotel doctor, and right away he asked if she had had anything to drink. She had not, but she did have a temperature and was all broken out like the measles from food poisoning. Our three friends stayed with us, missed all the tours, but did watch the New Years's Eve celebration from our window (probably just as well). Soon it started to snow—pretty great big flakes.

On New Year's Day in the evening we did go to a dinner, where Dr. Finley, editor of *The Times*, was the speaker. We felt honored to meet him. We also took a tour of The Times Building.

We were luckier when it came to our return voyage, for we had a new modern boat, the George Washington. We enjoyed seeing other boats all lit up at night passing us, and we thought of Mother quoting "Ships That Pass in the Night." It was an uneventful trip home, and we arrived late at night, tired but feeling that we had had a new and rewarding experience.

Those School Tours

When we took that tour in 1934 to New York, the teachers and advisers of school papers had some of their students along, but nobody got lost. It's different now.

The year we retired my sister and I both had letters from different companies painting in glowing terms the pleasures of a trip by boat to the Mediterranean and to Rome. It would benefit our Latin pupils they claimed. Now the boys and girls might have enjoyed it, but would I? Would the worries outweigh the pleasures? Some of the students might get lost down in the Catacombs or exploring the Coliseum, trying to see where they kept the lions. They always did like that story of "Androcles and the Lion." I didn't show them the literature. They would have said, "Why can't we?" to their parents and to me.

Our Civics teacher and sponsor of the Student Council did take a group on the bus to Washington, D.C. one year. She didn't have any trouble with the pupils, but she herself sustained a broken leg when she missed a step on the bus.

I Was Sure I saw
That Boy come
in Here!

Just this year I had a letter from her (now retired like me) in which she recounted the troubles some of the sponsors had on a trip to Williamsburg this spring. It seems one of the girls eluded them and got part way to California, but couldn't go all the way with only $75.00. Last year my cousin, who teaches English, history, and civics in a California school, brought one student to observe Congress in session. I guess there wouldn't be much danger of that girl getting lost.

A Call for Help

"Save me! Save me!" That call for help broke the silence of my nice, quiet noon hour. I was sitting at my desk eating my lunch. I looked up just in time to see one of my homeroom boys in the doorway at the back of my room. He was a fat roly-poly, chubby little seventh grader and he was all out of breath from running.

I didn't know what I was supposed to save him from, but I pushed my chair back, and he dived under my desk and nestled there at my feet. I looked up again and saw one of my co-workers, a tall heavy-set woman, who said, "I was sure I saw that boy come in here!"

I acted surprised but didn't say anything. After looking in my two cloakrooms along the side of the room, she went out. She did not come near my desk.

After a short lull my little culprit came up out of hiding, and I asked him what he had been up to. It seemed he was in the hall by her room and looked in her door, at the front of her room. She was eating her lunch, and he just couldn't resist shooting a paper wad. His aim was good and it went whizzing right past her nose. I gave him a little lecture, and then urged him to stay on the playground in the good fresh air during the noon hour. Teachers deserved a little quiet and peace.

A Valentine

"You made me what I am today!" So said a "Valentine for Teacher" that was left on my desk one fine day in February. I was ready to pat myself on the back but did not know who left it.

VALENTINE
For
TEACHER
I owe Everything to you!
your Student
OVER →
THANKS

cocky; I turned it over to see who
me. There was a picture of a convict
ing on a bench in his cell with the

rd says a lot to us who deal with
mic one I remember receiving, but
ved and kept in a prominent place
t school for the children to see, for
l).
re I can put my hands on it without
een guilty of sending anyone down
kful not only to that cartoonist but
no left it for me to find.

the Navigator

s after learning to drive, we drove
to see the World Exposition. Then
ey and to Arcata, where our aunt
from home there had been one dis-
driving in Tennessee and in passing
too soon and got the right rear fender dented. She
felt bad about it, but the two ladies in the other car were very
gracious. Their car didn't even get a scratch and no one was hurt.

Nevertheless Elsie said she would study the maps and let
me do the driving. I enjoyed driving but now I realize I should
have insisted on her taking the wheel again. Years later after
I had knee surgery, she saw the need and started practicing
on a Kroger vacant lot (extra parking space used generally only
on Saturdays). She surprised me one day when she ventured
out on a four-lane street. From then on she was driving again
and very happy.

Elsie piloted me through Los Angeles and through Oakland
to Berkeley. I remember with gratitude a policeman during
the rush hour on San Pablo Boulevard who pulled me out of
a cross street by stopping traffic. He must have seen our big
front W. Va. license and figured there was a scared or green
driver behind the wheel.

We stayed at Napa all night and nearly froze after being so
hot crossing the desert. The next morning I was so pleased to

ERRATA

p.7 - at end of quotation
From Holmes - "sea" - not
seal.

p.73 - comparative
philology - not philosophy.

p.133 - asked, "what are
you - not your.

take a picture of a "deer" by the side of the road, but when I got the picture developed it was a goat. Such a disappointment!

After a visit with our relatives we headed north along the coast, and here again Elsie studied the maps and schedules for the ferry boats across five wide estuaries on the Oregon Coast, and had it figured out just right so we didn't have long waits for the ferry.

I wasn't so skillful in my picture taking. With my camera I took all those ferries, scenes in Portland and up the Columbia River. When we had the film developed at home I found I had put the roll back in the camera, so that we had double exposures. I couldn't get the ferries again, because the next time we went that way, there were five new bridges.

Flood Refugees

The week beginning January 24, 1937 will go down in history as a disastrous time on account of the floods on the Ohio River, and it will be forever etched in my memory not only from reading and hearing about it, but from my actual involvement with taking care of flood refugees.

Besides the flood, there was a bad fire in Cincinnati. Gasoline on the water was ablaze, and that in turn had set fire to the Crosby Building, causing the radio announcers to flee. On the 24th the water was over the sixty-foot wall in Portsmouth, and the next day it was eighty feet above flood stage at Cincinnati. Radios were given over entirely to news bulletins, and ham radio operators were busy doing their part to help in the rescue efforts.

On January 26 about 2000 refugees came from Huntington 50 miles away to be placed in our school buildings. At first we at Lincoln Junior High got 100 and later 50 more. The home economics teachers did most of the cooking, but I was given an easy job, scrambling eggs at 6:00 A.M. for their breakfast and serving them in the large gym, where cots and tables had been set up. Later in the day I peeled onions and carrots for lunch. I remember going uptown to buy a smock to wear while working.

Another job that was given me was taking care of the children in our big study hall. I liked that. Another teacher and I passed out clothing, dolls, marbles, and toys that we had purchased uptown. We also took them walking around the school block. Some teachers helped the refugees take showers and get rid of their muddy clothes. Other teachers had charge of the infirmary in our art room, where the sick people were, but they soon had a nurse in charge there. At one time I held a four-week old baby.

One of our older teachers, who was directing us, had to quiet a woman who was screaming continuously. The teacher reverted to the kind of language the woman evidently was used to in her locality and said to her, "You believe in the Lord, don't you? Yes! Well He ain't pleased with ya now!" The woman quieted down.

My sister also helped at her building. We both felt happy that we could do a little to help. On February 3 the refugees started for home. It was the worst flood in history on the Ohio from Pittsburgh, Pennsylvania, to Cairo, Illinois. It took two days to clean the buildings, so Elsie and I took advantage of the free time to go to a theater to see pictures of the flood (no T.V. in those days).

In 1937 we spent most of the summer on the beach at Big Lagoon, California, only two miles from Patrick's Point, our favorite agate hunting ground. Our aunt rented a cottage there, and we helped her furnish it.

Sometimes, when we went down the steep trail to the Point, Mother sat in the parked car at the head of the trail in a clear spot, where she could see us down on the beach. She enjoyed the beautiful scenery and visiting with other people. One day some strangers asked her how to identify agates. She said, "See those two girls down there wearing white beach hats? They are my daughters. They can tell you."

We wondered why we had had so many people coming up to us that day and asking, "Is this an agate?"

If we had to tell them it wasn't we usually gave them some of ours for samples.

Another time, when the beach was all fine sand, and we knew there wouldn't any be agates, because it takes a heavy wave or strong tide to roll the pebbles in, we were looking out the picture window in the cabin and saw a group of children arriving with their leader. Elsie noticed our basket of agates

Remember
the Harpies!
Do they want the
glass ball?

on the table and said, "When they get far enough away so they won't see us, let's scatter these rocks on the beach." So we hurried down the path and threw them around but not all in one place. Then we watched at the window.

Sure enough, before long they had turned and were coming back. As soon as they came upon these "planted" rocks you should have seen the excitement. First one and then another picked one up and went running up to their leader to show it. They were happy, and I know we were.

At night we could hear the pounding of the surf and often saw phosphorescence on the water. We tried not to think about the possibility of an earthquake or of a tidal wave, while we were so close to the water with those big waves coming in.

We were really in more danger when we went out on the lagoon in a motor boat with a twelve-year-old boy. His family had just bought the boat, and he had not taken it out by himself before, but he asked his mother, and she said "Yes." We went almost out of sight, and our mother, as well as his, was very uneasy. Fortunately the wind did not come up, and we came back, to the relief of everyone watching. That was just another time when we regretted that we had not taken swimming lessons in high school, where we had a pool right in the building.

Elsie did have a scary experience one day when some big birds came diving down over her head from the cliffs above. She was so excited because she had found one of those glass fishnet floats that the Japanese used on their fishing boats before the war. She did not wait for our aunt to bring her back in the car but walked the five miles on that deserted beach to our cabin. The birds (I think they were pelicans) did not like this intrusion on their nesting ground. That made us think of the Harpies that Aeneas had to contend with in the Trojan war story.

Seventh Trip to California

Although we'd already had six trips to California, the seventh one was really outstanding. Each trip had something unique to be remembered years later. I recall this 1938 train trip as giving us a most inspiring mental picture.

The last night before we were due to arrive in Berkeley, we went to bed early in our Pullman berths. Elsie and I usually bought a section and instead of pulling the upper berth down to be made up, we slept together on the lower (crowded to be sure but cozy and comfortable). Mother had a section next to us.

About midnight we woke up and looked out on the most beautiful scene. We were up high in the Sierras, and the deep snow came right up to the tracks. The big bright full moon made dark shadows of every pine tree. There was a red beacon light blinking over a distant field, and our train was just gliding along noiselessly. It was like being up in a plane, I imagine. (I have never been up.) The only sounds were made by the train going through an occasional snowshed.

It was a sight to treasure and all three of us stayed awake for an hour, watching it for it was truly entrancing. I thought about those poor pioneers who had perished at Donner Pass and then thought how grateful we should be for our nice, warm, comfortable train.

In the morning we got up about 5:00 so that we could be ready to get off at Berkeley. Yes, we were coming back to work on our M. A. degrees. We had taken three courses in Latin earlier, but found no more Latin offered in summer. In 1932 our professor of Latin had become president of the University, even giving up an opportunity to be a visiting professor in Rome. He was the third Westerner to be so honored, the other two having been from Stanford.

We changed our major to education but were able to do our seminar studies (really like theses) in a subject related to teaching Latin. Our Schools had closed early at home that year, and that gave us a chance to attend both the intersession and the summer session (twelve weeks).

When we arrived in Berkeley we took a taxi to the University and went to three classes. Mother registered at the Berkeley Inn and then went apartment hunting. She found the Ambrosia Apartments where we stayed until Mother left for her home and we transferred to International House for the next six weeks.

Hindustani

Who would have thought that we would ever know any Hindustani? (I don't now.) This story shows another advantage of being a twin. We started the summer term that year with a test in recognizing Hindustani words that was sprung on us the first day in our statistics class. The test was on recognizing Hindustani words. Now my sister and I were always intrigued by words and comparative philosophy, but this time the words were just "hen scratches." We were given five minutes to look at them and their meanings with the expectation of trying to remember them the next week when we came to class.

We stared at them and the English but could see no connection. On the way home we talked about them. "Did you notice that one that looked like a chair?" I asked.

"Yes, and there was one that looked like a ladder," she said. (Now I don't recall what they meant, but then I did.)

The next week we surprised ourselves in that we remembered enough to make the top scores. (It didn't count on our grades—just an experiment.) The other students asked, "How did you remember any of those funny looking words!" We really didn't know, unless it was "by association" and our talking about them.

This test was given by the professor of statistics to see if there was correlation in learning the two subjects. The answer was negative, but it might have been positive, if I had not carelessly forgotten to copy some of my answers from the back to the front of the page. However, at the end of the term I redeemed myself (let me brag a little here) by making 100 on the final test, which took three hours and seven pages of paper to finish.

International House Again

We were happy to be back in I House again where we met some former friends. Most of the days were spent in study, but nearly every Saturday we went to San Francisco for sightseeing, and Sunday afternoons we went to the band concerts in Golden Gate Park.

Prices were still very reasonable; for example, Elsie had soup, rare rib of beef, shrimp salad, fruit punch, and chocolate cream roll, all for sixty cents at a large cafeteria.

On July 24, 1938, coming back to Oakland, we had a thrill in seeing the U.S. Fleet on the Bay. We counted twenty-four battleships, but here were sixty-three. President Roosevelt was to review them from 2:00 to 4:00 P.M., and all ferries were to stop running. We got the last one back at 2:00. Each ship gave a twenty-one gun salute as the president passed by, and it sounded like thunder all afternoon.

We enjoyed our seminar group very much. It was just a small class and the professor always said, "We'll call on the twins first," and generally Elsie punched me to go ahead. We liked to look for similar studies in the library, and Elsie was pleased when she discovered that our own superintendent in Charleston had studied the relation of Latin to the social studies, whereas hers was to be on mathematical terms from the Latin. That winter she sent and got his study to review it, as we had to do with several others.

At International House two colored ladies, teachers from Washington, D.C., lived across the hall from us, and they were very friendly. They lent us books and invited us into their front room to watch the Fourth of July fireworks over the Bay. They came across the hall to help me, when I was sick and were always jolly. I remember them saying, "We have our E.S. degrees."

We asked, "What does that mean?"

They replied, "Eminently Superior!"

Final Session of Summer School

After working on our seminar studies for a whole year at home, sending off for similar studies, typing data, etc. We started for California again on June 12, 1939. This time we felt rather sad, for we knew that we would finish our work and after that we would miss the excitement of registering, going into new classes, and meeting people.

Mother had decided to stay with us, so we got the same apartment in Berkeley that we had had for six weeks the previous year. The landlady welcomed us and gave us a guide to the World's Fair. We had come a week early to have time to go to Treasure Island to enjoy the Fair, before we started our studies. We rented a typewriter and pounded it all day.

Mother enjoyed doing the marketing and preparing our meals.

Every day we went to the Fair, but the greatest pleasure we had was riding in a trolley car across San Francisco Bay over the new bridge. It was just like flying to look down on the Bay and Treasure Island, where the Fair was located—or like looking down on a relief map such as the one we used to look at in the old Ferry Building. Now there was a new rail terminal at the end of the bridge, but we did have to get a ferry over to the Island. The sixty-three battleships were in the harbor again and looked so pretty all lit up at night, as we were returning to Berkeley. The colored lights of the Fair covered the whole Island and made it look like fairyland.

One of the outstanding exhibits at the Fair we found in a building called Sermons from Science. The speaker said that everything we said was recorded in the rocks, or environment around us and that we could hear Julius Caesar's voice, if we only had the key to unlock it. The demonstrations on light and color were marvelous too.

Most of the Fourth of July we spent in the library, a safe enough place, as we told one professor, when he cautioned us to be careful on this holiday. On the 5th we went to San Francisco to attend sessions of the NEA being held there that year. Our professor in educational policies, Dr. William G. Carr, had excused the class, so we we could all go.

Elsie and I went to the meeting of the American Classical League and met some of the authors of textbooks we had used. They all made excellent talks, but the best one was given by Dr. R.D. Harriman, from Stanford, on "Quintillian Among the Moderns." I was so inspired by his talk that I spent the next three weeks in the library reading Quintillian every spare minute I had.

Although a Spaniard by birth, Quintillian wrote in Latin and taught in the first century in what is called the first Roman public school. His *Institutio Oratoria* gives advice to classroom teachers that is good today. For example, he advocated what we call "reading readiness" where the teacher will stoop to the child's level, just as in walking with a small child he will give him his hand and adjust his speed to that of his little companion.

In our class in supervision I mentioned some of these "modern" practices advocated so long ago, such as motivation and provision for individual differences. Dr. Merton E. Hill, an outstanding educator, who not only taught at U.C. but commuted every weekend to teach a large Bible class in Pasadena, was pleased with that report and said they ought to read Quintillian in the high school Latin courses.

The first day we were in his class he asked us all to tell where we were from and what we taught. After my sister and I answered this "roll call," he said, "We are so happy to have you come clear across the continent to study with us. I never knew a Latin teacher who wasn't just in love with her work."

My sister and I had never been so warmly welcomed before, and we worked like mad to do well. He was on our committee for the oral exam, the only professor on it that we knew, and you can imagine how glad we were.

July 31 was the big day. Elsie had her oral test first at 9:00 A.M. She missed one question—"When was the stamp of approval put on geometry?" Her study had to do with the usefulness of Latin vocabulary in the study of geometry. Mine was on how well the textbooks conformed to the recommendations of the Classical Investigation.

My oral exam was at 11:00 and I too missed one question— "What was the first Latin textbook published in this country?" I know that now, even to this day—Hale's.

In Dr. Carr's class on the last night, one of the students, beginning his report said, "War has started!" We did not know what he was talking about, but he was right. In a short time, only two years, we were in World War II, and we who had lived in peace and harmony in International House among all nationalities couldn't understand how that could be. (I still don't.)

In Dr. Williams' class we finished the seminar studies we had been working on for two years. I remember walking through the campus late at night to go over our copies with the stenographer, but we weren't afraid then, even though it was very dark with all those trees on the campus. The last night we were there Dr. Williams and his wife gave a party for the class, and when we left he was full of emotion, for he was retiring that year. He patted Elsie on the shoulder and said, "Good-bye, little girl." We were sad too.

PS. Those seminar studies are resting on library shelves somewhere out there at U.C. I hope someone has had occasion to refer to them.

We stayed a week after the session closed so that we could meet Mother's two sisters as well as our cousin Betty and her friend. We went to the Fair with them. We had already been there, so we knew the best places to take them, but even then we kept getting lost from one another and had to go on a hunt for the "lost" one. I finally sat in a conspicuous place and let them come and find me.

Navigator Again

Elsie was "navigator" on the train too, as well as when we were traveling by car. She followed the timetable closely and always knew just what the next stop would be and when we were due. It was a good thing, because she could sometimes help other travelers.

I remember the night we left Berkeley, Calfornia, in 1939 for home. There was a large crowd, some waiting in the station and others standing outside. We noticed three women looking our way and finally two of them came up to us. One of them said to me, "Would you mind looking after my aunt here and showing her when to get off the train? She is a deaf mute."

I said I'd be glad to, knowing that Elsie could do it. The woman got on the train with us and sat across the aisle. Elsie watched the schedule, and a few minutes before we were due at the lady's station motioned for her to get up, helped her into her wraps, saw that her baggage was ready and all set to go, when the conductor came back for her. The train made a very short stop. We watched from our window and were relieved to see some folks there to meet her.

My question is this. What made them choose us out of all that crowd? I was glad Elsie was there with her timetables.

An Unexpected Vacation

In August 1940, just before time for school to open, there was an epidemic of infantile paralysis in our state with 150 cases reported. Therefore the opening of school was postponed until the last of September, and the West Virginia State Fair was canceled.

Since my sister and I had both had polio, there would be no risk to anyone if we took a little trip. We had had a long hot summer, listening to the depressing news about the war in Europe. We actually heard the air raid sirens broadcast from London.

We delayed starting on our trip, because on September 3 President Roosevelt, Secretary Ickes, and other celebrities were coming through Charleston to inspect the Naval Ordnance Plant in South Charleston, where $20 million had been appropriated to expand the plant. The procession included Governor Holt and many dignitaries riding in thirty-five cars, and as they sped along on our boulevard, which was only two blocks from our house, we had a good chance to see them. We waved, as did the others in the crowd, and they waved back, giving us a thrill.

Although the weather was bad in the East on account of a hurricane along the coast, we decided to go and headed for Vermont. A picture in our paper showed the railroad station at Marshall, North Carolina, under water. We remembered that place very well, for we had stayed there on our way to Asheville and had worried all night on account of the rising water.

Also in the news on radio we had heard President Roosevelt the day before he came to Charleston dedicate the Chickamauga Dam and then, at Newfound Gap, the Great Smoky Mountain National Park.

In contrast to the heat at home, we nearly froze all the way to the Canadian border, but we did have some gorgeous scenery. We had a thrill when we came down Bear Mountain and saw the Hudson River. I turned the wrong way on the highway, and Elsie, the good navigator, informed me we were going south to the city. That's just what I didn't want with all that traffic.

After getting turned around we had some terrific driving at 15 miles per hour (as posted) up the Storm King Highway to West Point. We stayed in a court at Newburgh, where crabapples falling on the roof bombarded us all night. We did not know until the next morning what had caused the noise.

In the Adirondacks we had hard driving too, with low gear required down Tongue Mountain to Lake Sunday and Lake George. It was historical as well as beautiful country, especially around Lake Chaplain and Fort Ticonderoga.

We had a little worrisome experience at some cabins at Chimney Corner on the Canadian border. I drove across into Canada just to say I had driven there. The customs officer was so agreeable to let me do this. When we came back to the Court, we went into the restaurant and sat in a booth, putting our three purses up on the window sill. It was late in the season, and there were no other customers. Soon a big, burly, rough-looking man came in and sat across from us, all the while glaring at our purses. He called out to the girl in the front room, "Bring me a cup of coffee!"

Just then a big dog came in and sat at the end of our table. We felt protected and hurried to finish our meal. When Elsie paid the cashier in the other room, she asked her if she had sent the dog in; she said, "No." The dog stood right by us as we were paying and walked out the door with us to our cabin. We were thankful for that dog. Perhaps we should not have been afraid, but we had vivid imaginations and could imagine some prisoner of war escaping across the border, since England was sending their war prisoners to Canada.

Police Escort

In 1941 we started out for a little trip and ended up out on the Pacific Coast. We called our aunt in Northern California, and she was surprised. In Tacoma, Washington, where we stayed all night in a motor court I had a little work done on my car; I had been worrying about its performance crossing the deserts. As we were a little early arriving, we decided to have the car serviced, but didn't know what way to go.

On a corner at one intersection I spotted a policeman, and since the light was red, I called out and asked him if he could direct us to the Packard garage. He came right over (it was near quitting time for him) and said, "I'll take you there—just follow me."

I did and had to be fast at the wheel to keep up, not knowing when we were making a turn, but he did give good signals and drove right into the Service Department and spoke to the foreman for us.

That was the only time I ever had a police escort (except in a funeral procession).

War Years

It is worthy of note that we lived through two world wars and the conflicts in Korea and Vietnam. We were in school during World War I as mentioned in a previous chapter but were teaching during World War II. My sister and I, like the other teachers, were involved in wartime activities, such as rationing, selling Victory Bonds, conducting paper drives, and writing letters to the soldiers.

It was a time of high patriotism, and the youngsters participated enthusiastically. They went out after school collecting tinfoil, paper and whatever was needed. They were so proud to bring it in the next morning and deposit it in boxes in our halls. My sister found a "gold mine" when she sorted through some papers. She came upon an old *Etude* magazine that had the music for *Der Fledermaus* (The Bat) in it. Delighted, she brought it home to try it on our piano. (I guess she would be forgiven for taking that one page.)

As things began to get scarce, we heard talk of rationing such as they already had in Europe. So in February 1943, the teachers went to classes one day to learn how to do rationing. The next day we were in our respective buildings passing out books of stamps for coffee, then for meat and later gasoline. There were some unexpected delays because they might have unusually long lines at one school, like ours, and then we would send someone to borrow more books from some other school not so rushed. We had to keep accurate records, of course. I recall one man got angry at me, because I couldn't give him more stamps. I had to follow directions.

We had "Banking Tuesday" at school in our homeroom. The pupils could bring a little money to put in their "very own bank accounts." I wonder if the bank tellers didn't get weary counting those pennies. Also we sold "War Stamps" and "Victory Bonds," later known as E Bonds.

The most vivid memories of those years had to do with

BOMB SCARE

Only Room for Two

"blackouts" and bomb scares. I can still hear those whistles and sirens. We had inspectors who came to the door if there was the least bit of light showing. We took this seriously and it's good we did, for Charleston is in what is called "Chemical Valley" with the big Carbide plant at the west end and Du Pont on the east.

One day when the bomb scare siren sounded, it was cold weather and we were in school, but we had to get out anyway. The teacher had to be last out of the room; so as I came to the door, I grabbed my fur (dyed muskrat) coat off the hook in my little closet. Our patrol boys were out at all four corners of the block, for the school took a whole block, and they held up their "Stop!" signs. The traffic stopped too. (Those boys were so proud to do this.) Pupils and teachers had to wait across the street. As we were standing there I noticed one little girl shivering and looking at me. I raised my right arm and she came right in under my coat. Then another came on the other side, so that I felt like a mother hen protecting her chicks with her wings.

December 7, 1941, was the most memorable day of that whole period. We had taken Mother out for a short drive in the country that quiet Sunday afternoon. When we got home, our phone was ringing, and a friend said, "Turn on your radio."

We did, and you know what we heard—excited voices of news reporters and the bad news about Pearl Harbor. Peace and quiet were a thing of the past. From then on it was listening to the radio day and night, but we didn't have the worries that many other people did, for we had no men the right age to go to war.

Mother, being English, had been listening all along (while we were in school) to the reports from Europe. I don't think she ever missed one of Winston Churchill's talks. In the Pacific area, she had first cousins and an aunt in Hawaii. Later her aunt came back to the States, but the cousins remained on the island.

Rose Bowl Canceled

The Rose Bowl game was canceled, but Duke invited Oregon State to come east and play in Durham, North Carolina, We were especially interested in that game, because Mother had a first cousin, whose son, Don Durdan, had been leading his team from Oregon State to victory all season. We could not go to the game, held on New Year's Day in 1942, but we sent Don a telegram the night before. We did listen on the radio and heard his name called out frequently, identifying him as that "left-handed, quarterback." It was a close game and Oregon State won, which pleased us.

We remembered Don as that little twelve-year old boy who had bothered us by throwing firecrackers near our heels while we were walking on the beach in California twelve years before on the Fourth of July.

Years later I mentioned that game to a friend who had gone to Duke. He said he was right there sitting in the rain and watching their team getting defeated by that quarterback.

End of the War

For me the end of World War II is not only a matter of reading about it in history, but something to recall, as we had lived through those exciting days. D Day and VJ Day bring up vivid memories.

Early on the morning of June 6, 1944, we were awakened by the paper boys calling out, "Extra! Extra!" Elsie got up and bought one and then turned on the radio. It was 5:30 and we kept it on all day, as the news broadcasts were continuous. The Allies had landed on the coast of France shortly after midnight. President Roosevelt had written a 500-word prayer for us to repeat with him at 10:00 that night. He had also reported the Allied occupation of Rome the previous day.

August 14, 1945, was another exciting day. Again we were awakened by the cries of "Extra! Extra!"; at 4:30 A.M. the sirens were blowing, although President Truman's official announcement of the surrender of the Japanese did not come until that evening. It set off tremendous celebrations everywhere. In our neighborhood one man started shooting and the children somehow found some firecrackers. Two of our local radio stations had devotional programs. (Note: On August 17 I bought my first unrationed gasoline, and took a drive to Marmet, ten miles up the river and back.)

At 9:30 P.M. on September 1 we listened on the radio to an eyewitness description of the surrender ceremonies aboard the Missouri. President Truman officially proclaimed September 2 as VJ Day. Although it was time for rejoicing, we had already celebrated it, just as we had celebrated D Day in 1944, as soon as the end of the war was assured. It was an occasion for both sadness and joy, but especially for giving thanks to God for the end of the conflict.

PART III
TEACHING CONTINUED

After the War—Looking Forward

The end of World War II in 1945 coincided with the halfway mark in our lives together, for we were forty-one that year. We tried to look forward to something new each day.

> "Umquam prorsum
> Numquam retrorsum!"

That was a good motto for us to follow: "Ever forward, never backward!"

It would seem, since we had finished the work for our degrees, that we no longer had a challenge to face. Such was not the case. We had time now to polish rocks and study mineralogy, to do volunteer work, etc.

(Of course, we had forty little challenges in each class every day.)

In 1985 we had a table in the Arts and Crafts show and enjoyed explaining things to people as they passed by.

It has been said, "Life begins at forty," and that has proved true in a way, but we certainly had a full life before we were forty. We had not realized all of our dreams, but that kept us hoping—hoping for new and better things, like ways to inspire others to see the beauty in nature and not "pass by with unrewarded eye," as Lowell would say.

My Writing Career

"Seek not for words, seek only fact and thought,
And crowding in will come the words, unsought."

Horace

My writing career, like Stephen Leacock's "financial career," has been very short. I'll tell you how I was launched into print. It was very simple. The morning after commencement exercises at school, I realized that my class of 9As had gone forever from my room. Just the week before, I had been counting the days, the hours—yes, even the minutes till I would be free from them, but now I would gladly have called them all back. Only a person who has worked, worried, played, laughed, and lived with a group of lively teenagers for three years can appreciate how I felt. That night I couldn't sleep, for thinking about the vacant chairs, and the thoughts came "crowding in" (as in the quotation above) so fast that I got up and scribbled a "story."

The next morning, by mere coincidence, my principal, seeing my downcast look, asked, "Why don't you write something for publication?"

I replied, "I have," and pulled my "story" out of my purse. As he read, I watched his expression and was pleased when he laughed. If he was disappointed that it was not a scholarly dissertation, he graciously concealed it. He put it in his pocket and said he wanted to show it to his wife.

In August I was surprised to receive a letter from *Clearing House* magazine in New York saying that the proofs of my story, "It's a Bee," were being sent to me, as my story would be in the September issue. I shall never feel so important again, but now my worries began and I hurriedly looked up my old scratched-up copy. I wondered if I had been too frivolous. We had used that magazine in our education classes and I recalled it was very scholarly.

Perhaps you are wondering about the title, "It's a Bee." To explain, I'll quote the first paragraph:

"It's a bee, children!" That is what I kept saying when a big bumblebee came buzzing into my room disrupting the quiet (?). Don't these junior high boys and girls know a bee? Of course they do, but my remark is not meant for them. It is directed toward one corner of the room, where, if you look

closely, you will see a small, inconspicuous black box conceal-
ing a loudspeaker, and my remark is meant for that unsen
person (our principal), who may be tuning in to my room over
our newly installed intercommunication system at this most
inopportune time. I tell the class in Latin to keep quiet *(Silete!)*,
hoping that my pupils will understand my Latin and that he
has forgotten his. He won't know that those shrill squeaks and
shrieks are caused by the girls when the bee comes near them
or that those loud slams are made by the books that the boys
are throwing at it in an attempt to kill it. (Footnote: Of course,
in the story later on I did point out the good features of an
intercom system.)

Elsie as Navigator Again

In 1948 Uncle Frank and Aunt Elsie came to visit us. He
was a good driver, but being used to wide, open spaces he
didn't like traffic. He had a peculiar way of getting to a certain
city by following a bus. For example, on their way East he
saw a bus marked Memphis and just followed it, because he
knew from there he could probably follow another bus coming
east to West Virginia.

He succeeded in getting to our home and from there on,
Elsie was there with her maps. We went with them to Cape
Cod and then to St. John, where Mother and Aunt Elsie were
born. When he got to New York, he wanted to stay at a motel
in New Jersey overnight and go through New York City in
the early morning. The trouble with that was that we got
mixed up with that heavy truck traffic. We finally got on the
George Washington Bridge, and Elsie, sitting up front, tried
to direct him. We got on the Henry Hudson Parkway and as
we came to a toll gate, Elsie said, "Ask the man for directions."

Frank was so elated at getting out of the city that all he
said was, "Is this the way out of this here country?"

That didn't help a bit, but Elsie on a pure hunch said,
"Turn right here," and that proved to be right, for in a few
minutes we saw a sign "To Merritt Parkway," just where we
wanted to be, according to Elsie. I didn't know. I never knew
where we were.

We found the only trouble with being on parkway (later

interstates) there were no restaurants. We had started out without any breakfast. We finally found a place where some college boys were in charge, and they kept beating those fried eggs down with a turner as if they were using an old-fashioned carpet beater on some rugs. Anyhow they tasted good even if they were all hard and crisp and looked like frilly straw hats.

We had a hard time to get Uncle Frank to stop for anything. (He was making time.) We saw lobster pounds and cooked lobsters for sale but could not get any. Just before we entered the city of St. John, New Brunswick, we did buy a lobster. Before that we had visited a granite quarry, and the "rock-hounds" had to buy some samples. When it came time to eat our lobster we chose a big chunk of granite to pound the legs open. Since we were out on the porch of the motel the girls in the restaurant nearby saw us. When we went down for dinner they said, "We saw you pounding on that lobster on the porch railing." I suppose they wondered how we could order a chicken dinner, when we had just feasted on lobster.

In St. John Mother showed us the house where she had lived, and seeing an elderly man nearby, she asked him if he had ever known Thomas Durdan (Mother's father).

"Oh, yes," he said. "I bought his furniture, when he moved to California."

That had been forty-four years ago, and Mother was glad to talk with him, but still it made her a little sad. When we looked at the Reversible Falls near the mouth of the St. John River, she told us about a boat that she was on when it got disabled and started drifting toward the Falls. They were rescued by the crew of another boat. When the tide is in there is not much of a waterfall, for the tide causes the river to rise and flow upstream.

On our way to Halifax we stopped at a court in Parrsboro. We were so cold at midnight we got up and put sweaters on over our nightclothes even though we had four blankets. A little meadow lark had ben cheeping all night. In the morning Frank picked it up and warmed it in his hands.

When we came home, we found *The National Geographic* in our mail and were interested in seeing a story with pictures of people finding agates in that stream in Parrsboro, right where we had been.

Later after we moved into the Village, we met a resident who gave us some little fossils with fern imprints on them, which she had found also in that locality. She did tell us, however, that she slid all around over those slippery rocks and had to wear rubber boots. That's not for us!

In Halifax we went to the Citadel and then by ferry and bus down to the beach, where we saw lobster pounds. Aunt Elsie did not go but spent the afternoon in a Woolworth's store. Returning from Halifax to St. John we stopped at Moncton to watch for the Tidal Bore to come in. We waited an hour and got eaten up by mosquitoes. That same evening we drove seven miles out of our way to go to the Magnetic Hill.

In Frederickton we saw the church Mother attended and the house where she lived while she was in normal school. Our visit to Quebec, Ottawa, Montreal, and Toronto were full of adventure for us, for we had never been there before.

In Quebec we went through the Parliament buildings and the shrine, St. Anne de Beaupre. When we saw the Plains of Abraham, Mother remembered her history and told us about the English general, James Wolfe, who with his troops scaled the heights to defeat the French general, Louis Montcalm, thereby capturing the city. Both Generals died in the battle, which was in 1759. General Wolfe, hearing someone read Gray's "Elegy" remarked, "Gentlemen, I would rather have written that poem than to take Quebec tonight."

Again in Ottawa we toured Parliament buildings and were thrilled to see some mounted police in their colorful uniforms on the grounds. Elsie and I took a bus to a museum, where we saw a wonderful display of gems and minerals. On Sunday we attended services in the "Kirk," which was across the street from the hotel. In Montreal I remember vividly the flock of cedar waxwings in the tree by the door of our court.

In Toronto, Uncle Frank let Mother and Aunt Elsie out at Eatons, a large store, while we went with him to hunt for the post office. He had his mail forwarded to towns along the way, but he made a mistake in choosing a city like Toronto because the traffic is always heavy in a large town and it's easy to get lost. We spent a whole hour walking to the new building and then to the old building down by the docks, because someone directed us wrong.

We felt as if we were home again when we got to Niagara Falls. We stayed overnight at a motel on the Canadian side and enjoyed seeing the colored lights on the Falls. When we crossed the river next morning at Rainbow Bridge the customs officer told us how to take a new boulevard around Buffalo. We followed the lake all the way to Erie.

We stayed in Cleveland all night and parted the next morning as Frank was "making time," in going straight for the West Coast. Mother, Elsie, and I had reserved seats on an air-conditioned bus, but the air-conditioning went off at noon ("out of order") so we were doubly happy to get home that afternoon, where we had our own cool air and could relax.

Now we could say that we had seen Canada coast to coast, because we had come home in 1929 from Vancouver, British Columbia, on the Canadian National Railroad. This time we were happy to be in a car, and could stop wherever we wished. There were so many interesting, historical things to see, we could only take in the high spots, but we were thankful for that.

Cape Cod Revisited

Although we had traveled through New England, when we accompanied our aunt and uncle on their trip to Canada, we still had much to see there. It is true we had driven out to Hyannis on Cape Cod and had stayed over night at Plymouth, but our visit was cut short. When my aunt asked, "What is that coiled-up rope doing on our floor over there by the window?" our Uncle Frank told her it was a fire escape. The hotel, which overlooked Plymouth Rock and the Bay, was over two hundred years old.

That settled it. The next morning early we left the hotel but did take time to stop at the Pilgrim burial ground, a church, and the site of the first fort before hurrying North. When we came to the Canadian border two days later, I was sitting up front and so rattled at sight of the uniform that the customs officer was wearing, I couldn't think when he asked where we were born. Elsie quickly piped up from the back seat, "Jefferson, Ohio!"

The next year, 1949, was unusually hot that summer. On the first day of August we headed for the Northeast, but would you believe it? A heat wave struck there just as we arrived. It was 110° in Boston, and to make matters worse, there were bad forest fires on Cape Cod. We stopped at Buzzards Bay and stayed a week. It was just too hot to move, and Mother wasn't well.

Elsie and I went exploring and brought Mother's evening meals back to her. One time we thought we needed a little exercise; so we started walking toward Onset Bay past some beautiful homes. Before long a huge, brown dog came bounding out and barked at us. That was the end of our walk. We just turned and retreated.

Another event, which showed how inexperienced I was, happened when we were trying to come back to our court, which we knew was on the right side of the road. I kept to the right and we found ourselves driving over the Bourne Bridge to the Cape. We turned and came back, but I still hadn't figured out what was wrong, for we went over that same bridge three times before I got it straight. That was before the day of the "cloverleaf," at least down in West Virginia.

Now, on the more serious side, we all three were overcome with awe and inspiration when we went back to the cemetery and saw some familiar names—names of people that we had studied about in history. We saw the John Alden house and the Miles Standish one as well as the grave of William Bradford. We walked to the old Pilgrim church and again felt admiration for those early settlers. We looked at the Rock where they landed and recalled Felicia Heman's poem "The Landing of the Pilgrim Fathers." (I was teaching Heman's poem one time when the school superintendent visited my class. He said that was his favorite poem and stayed the whole period.) As we stood near the Rock that day we also thought of the Pilgrims' reasons for braving the dangers of the ocean and that "stern and rock-bound coast." We agreed with the poet's conclusion, "Aye, call it holy ground."

Before the week was up we did have a chance to drive out on the Cape to the Point and to Wood's Hole. Here we thought of Henry David Thoreau and his studying of nature. Fortunately, the towns of Bourne and Sandwich were saved from the fire. Of yes, we read in the papers that the temperatures

DeLuxe Motor Court
And, We paid money for this!

were in the seventies in West Virginia. As far as weather was
concerned, we would have fared better to have stayed at home.
However, we were glad we took the trip, for we came a little
closer to the history of our country than we could have in
studying books.

An Experience with Spiders

On our return trip from New England, we came to Albany,
New York, and across to Erie, Pennsylvania, where we stopped
for the night. We selected a pretty motor court down near the
lake under some nice shade trees. This was on the east side of
town; we could see a storm gathering in the west and wanted
to get settled.

Around 8:00 the storm broke in all its fury. We looked
around in our cabin and saw spiders clinging to the rafters
everywhere. I guess the storm drove them in. Anyway we made
a dash to our car and sat in it till 11:00 when the storm abated
a little. We were dismayed when we saw that the roof of our
cabin was leaking and the water in the bathroom was all
muddy. We wouldn't even brush our teeth. Preparatory to
getting out early in the morning, we just lay down in the bed,
with our dresses on. Mother was on a single bed, not under
any drip, but Elsie and I had to put our umbrella up over our
heads and keep close together. Even at that I could just imagine
a big spider on the edge of the umbrella hanging down over
my nose. Elsie was afraid of the same thing on her side. Mother
just got a big laugh out of it and said, "Let's go to sleep."
How could we?

Early the next morning we started for home, and on the
other side of Erie we saw beautiful courts. Also we saw evidence
of the storm. There was a limb of a tree on a guard rail of a
bridge that had been under water. Some travelers from Ontario
told us that they couldn't get through to Erie during the night
at all. We had something to be thankful for even if we did
have spiders. (After that we never stopped where trees were
overhanging the roof.)

Clever Teenagers

Talk about youngsters being clever, we could recount many instances where they hit the mark with a clever saying. This is one I remember. My sister, who sponsored the school paper also had the yearbook, until some activities were curtailed on account of cost.

One year she brought home the "jingles" that were to go beside each picture in the book. There was one that we both laughed over, but she did not let it go in, for fear it might offend someone. The city and county schools had been recently consolidated. This is what the jingle editor had written about one of his classmates:

"J-B—, fresh from the sticks,
Came clomping in with the rest of the hicks."

Another time in our school the ninth graders in their Class Day program wanted to take off the teachers; so they asked to borrow a dress or suit from each of us. Most of us let them have something. There was one teacher noted for wearing the same outfit day after day. When the time came for the pupil wearing that teacher's dress to come on stage and the teacher's name was given, sure enough, a girl wearing that well-remembered green dress walked across the stage. A boy sitting next to me said so seriously, "Well, what is *she* wearing today?"

Florida Visited

Since our relatives all lived out West, when vacation time came we headed toward the West Coast, but one year, in 1951, we did go to Florida. Twenty years before, when we had gone to Atlanta with our father, he lamented that we did not go to Savannah or St. Augustine.

He would have enjoyed this trip, because he was interested in history and the Civil War. He had spent a long time looking at the cyclorama in Atlanta. We came into Charleston, South Carolina, over the high Cooper Bridge. That alone gave me a thrill. One thing I remember about Myrtle Beach was eating at the Pink House. I got so engrossed in reading one of Cicero's letters on the menu that I didn't see the waiter patiently standing at my elbow. Mother spoke up and said, "He's waiting for you to order."

Coming out, Elsie stood near the cash register to pay the bill but stepped back when a big bird (macaw) opened its bill (almost touching her ear). The next day we arrived at Savannah at noon and stayed overnight. We enjoyed the mockingbirds at the court, but not the red ants. After a week at Daytona we went on to St. Augustine. Eugenia Price had not written her books describing these places yet. Now, if we were going again we would enjoy looking for the places she mentioned.

After each little trip out from our court to see something like the oldest house or the first school house, we came back to the court to cool off. Probably the girls thought we were never going to check out.

In the hotel where we ate the evening before, we had to cut our meal short because the cooks wouldn't stay in the kitchen during a storm. We couldn't blame them, for the papers that day were full of news about tornadoes near Richmond, Virginia, the day before.

The worst storm we experienced was at West Palm Beach. When we came out of the Howard Johnson restaurant that evening, the sky was black to the west and a flock of birds was coming ahead of the storm. We just made it to the court, across the highway. The next morning we drove along the ocean at Palm Beach to see the trees and coconuts down.

When we reached Miami, we went a little farther south and visited a rare bird farm. That was interesting, but we should have taken along a bag of nuts, for those birds pecked at out ankles looking for food. Elsie kept swinging her purse to try to shoo them away.

For us, the outstanding features were seeing the wildlife, especially the flamingoes, the reptiles at the alligator farm, and the fish at Marine Land, where we were lucky in arriving just at feeding time.

As beachcombers, we looked for shells, Elsie's prize was a 50 cent piece, which was shining in the water at her feet. She kept it, like the "bear" rock from Yellowstone, in her souvenir box.

We came home through the mountains, but even then it was terribly hot. We didn't try to make time, usually stopping at noon. I don't know if we were welcome at the courts that early, but we did need to relax, review what we had seen, and plan for the next day.

Tornadoes

On all our trips West we had been lucky not to run into any bad storms, but in 1953 it was different. This was the last trip we had with Mother by train. We decided to go on the C & O Sportsman to Toledo, because it still made her sad to go through Cincinnati, as Father had always gone that far with us.

We left Charleston at 9:30 P.M., and when we woke up after leaving Columbus, the porter told us there had been six tornadoes killing over 100 people around Toledo. In the station we brought a paper to read about it. We felt so sorry for those people in it, we did not worry about being late. It seems that most of the injured were at a ball park and the strange thing was that those on one side of the road were not injured, whereas those on the opposite side were.

The New York Central train carrying one car of the California Zephyr, which started in New York, finally came through. We did get a thrill when we looked out our window and saw this train passing us and the silver CZ11 car right beside us. Since that was the train we were going to get on in Chicago, we asked the porter if we could transfer to it. He said he would take our bags and store them in that car so that we wouldn't have to bother with them in Chicago but that our car, CZ10, would be waiting there. That was a great help because we did have five bags.

In Chicago we discovered that CZ10 was the last car in a long train with part of our car being the observation car with the Vista Dome above it. We left at 3:30 P.M. and toward evening Elsie exclaimed, "Oh, look at the bright yellow sunset with black above it and below it!"

Mother said, "I don't like the look of that sky," but did not explain.

Elsie took the upper berth, and Mother and I were in the lower. About 9:30 our car being at the end was swaying. The engineer slowed down so that we were barely moving. Elsie got scared and came down to get in with Mother and me. She peeked out the window and said, "I see nothing but water—just like crossing Great Salt Lake!" We knew we weren't on any lake. Later, the conductor told us that we were the last train to get through Ottumwa, Iowa, as the tornado destroyed the station and tore up the tracks fifteen minutes after we got through. We were very thankful and stayed awake talking most of the night.

We went to breakfast at 6:00 and had lunch in the buffet lounge at noon. That evening we went into the diner according to a schedule. A Zephyrette took our reservations earlier in the day and then called us to tell us when to come. She was such an attractive girl in her light blue uniform and we enjoyed talking with her.

Elsie had a chance to do some more teaching in the diner. A young boy, who had just graduated from high school, sat with us at our table and asked, "What's this for?" when the waiter brought a service plate and his finger bowl. Elsie explained what they were. He got on the train at Ottumwa and had got away from the station like us just before the tornado struck.

In Denver we ran through the automatic train washer and we thought it was raining. We went through thirty tunnels including the six-mile long Moffatt tunnel. The scenery was beautiful all day, and we got so tired from looking and from lack of sleep the night before that we went to sleep early that evening and missed seeing Great Salt Lake.

The next morning we were up at 5:00 at Winnemucca and enjoyed seeing the Feather River Canyon, snow-capped peaks, and water falls. The conductor took delight in telling us all about everything. He said, "I have been on this run for forty-four years."

After a few days with our aunt in San Francisco, we went to her home in the redwood empire in Humboldt County and learned to cut and polish rocks on her lapidary equipment. We arrived home on August 21 and Mother was in the hospital on August 24 with double pneumonia. The air-conditioning was too much for her on the train from Chicago home.

Divine Intervention

When Mother, Elsie, and I were returning from our California trip we were so excited about getting home that we did not see or hear another train. When our eastbound train stopped, the engine was opposite the station, but we were in the last car, a Pullman at the far end, a long walk for us and there were no red caps. My sister, carrying her bag, forged ahead looking down at her feet and not hearing anything because of the roar of our engine. It was 3:35 A.M. and I had hold of Mother, who couldn't walk so fast.

All of a sudden, something told me to look up. I did and, to my horror, I saw the bright headlight of an engine coming toward us and Elsie heading for those tracks in order to cross over, as the station was on the side next to the river and our track was next to the ramp going up to the bridge overhead. I let go of Mother, yelled as loud as I could, "Elsie, stop!"

She looked around and I pointed to the train coming—just in time. She had not seen it or heard it. Ordinarily, there would not have been another train in the station at the same time, but on this occasion the Westbound George Washington was late. Now, what made me look up just then? To me it was more than just serendipity; it was "divine intervention" and I shall always be thankful.

Election Day

How to vote without offending anyone! That was the question that often bothered us on Election Day, especially in local elections. My sister and I usually had former pupils or other friends on the ticket. One year I had a student whose father was running for mayor, and I worked as a volunteer with his wife. On the other hand, we both knew the mother of the other candidate. She sat beside Elsie in church; so Elsie decided to vote for her son, while I voted for the other man. Of course, we killed one another's vote, but one of us could truthfully say, "Yes" to any questions, depending on who asked the question.

The biggest Election Day problem involved my sister, who had been asked to work at the polls. I never had that dubious honor, and it's a wonder she ever did again after that first experience. She got up early, too early for me, and went to the polling place to see what her duties were. She felt right at home because the voting was in her school building.

What she did not know was what to do about lunch, when the time came. She had noticed little white boxes being brought in and placed on a table near the door. When it was time to eat, several workers picked up their boxes of lunch. They contained fried chicken and a salad. She was hungry, so she got up and picked up a box. After she had finished her lunch, she noticed a man going over to the table, but there were no more boxes there. He asked, "Where's my lunch?"

Someone said, "Yours is gone."

Another spoke up and said, "Here come the Republicans now. Eat one of their lunches."

Then Elsie realized what she had done, and she was embarrassed, but there was nothing she could do about it then, so she just kept still. Those first boxes were for the Democrats, but how was she to know? She didn't know the politics of those around her.

The joke was that this man whose lunch she had taken, found, not chicken but a wiener in his Republican box. When she came home that evening, some of our Republican neighbors were there. She entertained us by telling about her "most embarrassing moment." They all laughed and one of them said, "It's a wonder you didn't choke on that Democrat chicken."

This Jet Age

Talk about people hurrying through life in this "jet age." We did it too in our day. When the alarm went off at 5:30 A.M. my sister and I jumped out of bed, jumped into our clothes, which had been laid out the night before, jumped up from the breakfast table (sometimes leaving the dishes) and hurried down to the car and jumped in. I took Elsie to her school and then went on to mine.

One morning she took my carryall by mistake into her building. It contained my lunch, as well as my papers, and, of course, I had hers. She called me up at school to tell me, and since we had a short time before the bell, I jumped back into the car and took her things to the door where she was waiting to get hers and give me mine. I surely would have missed that lunch.

Speaking of lunches, I am different from most people, for I like just plain buttered toast with coffee and some fruit. One morning I made my extra toast and packed my lunch before I ate. When I had gathered up my books, I looked everywhere for my lunch and finally called to Elsie, "Did you see my lunch anywhere?"

"Yes," she said, "You ate it."

That's right! My dear twin sister sat there at the table and saw me eating my school lunch and did not say a word. I had to grab a cookie and run—no time to make more toast.

Car Troubles

In 1955 we had car troubles and didn't go far from home. When a new car we bought had so many "bugs" to be taken out, we kept it only one year. Then we bought another new car, and it was the same story. In fact, I wrote about our problems and sent it to the company. In my letter I mentioned that I had made ninety trips back to the service department in the four months since we had bought the car. I remarked that the foreman and mechanics were very cooperative and tried hard to make repairs.

I told them that if the service foreman looked up from the counter some morning and did not see me sitting in my car waiting for him to put the door up, he would think it was Sunday and go home. Then I proceeded to spell out all the "illnesses" my car had had and concluded that the car had been made twice (once "half way" at the factory and again "hand-made" at the dealers.)

It had come off the assembly line so fast that some "nuts" couldn't hold on to a bolt and let it go down into the water pump, causing a terrible clatter just as we got to Manasquan, N.J. on the hottest day of the summer and with the traffic bumper to bumper. We managed to get a motel room at Sea Girt, where we waited three days for repairs.

When we got home we saw one of our neighbors driving

his pretty, big, new car out of our court one morning with lemons painted all over it. I was green about the meaning of those yellow lemons until someone explained to me what it meant.

I even bought *Hot Rod* magazine to see if I could learn something about a car. I took care to close the garage door, because I didn't want the boy who lived across the street to see his Latin teacher down on the floor of her garage with a flashlight trying to see what could be wrong with her car.

Elsie helped me look, too, one day when we had heard rocks hitting our car but didn't see anyone that could be throwing them. We saw the end of something up front hanging down, different from the other side. When I called the garage, they said, "Bring it up."

I said, "You come and get it. I'm not driving it through town falling apart."

Sure enough, when the service man saw it he asked, "Where are the parts?"

Parts? We didn't have any parts. They must be along the roadside. Later I think the man said it was the tie rod that had come loose.

So you can't blame me now for holding on to my good 1973 model and telling the salesman I was never going to sell it or trade it in.

Serendipity

Most words we don't remember just when we learned them, but I remember our minister one Sunday morning explained that serendipity meant fortunate chance happening that had not been planned. The word was coined by Horace Walpole in 1754 after a play, "Three Princes of Serendip," which had three heroes that made such happy discoveries. The minister gave examples showing how chance events can work out for one's good without planning.

When I thought about it, I could recall several such happenings. In fact, our lives have been full of serendipitous discoveries. The first one I thought about had happened a few days before that Sunday, when Mother was in the hospital. She was due to be dismissed from the hospital the next day and we had not been able to locate a nurse to stay with her. It just happened that we had a prescription for her to be filled at the drugstore. We told the clerk our trouble and she brightened right up and said. "I know a woman, my next door neighbor, who went off a case today and is free. I'll give you her phone number."

We were delighted and called her as soon as we got home. She said she would come the next day, and we had her for several months.

A Lucky Delay

One night when Mother was in the hospital in 1962, I started home at 11:00 as soon as her special night nurse came in. Since my aunt and her friend, May, were visiting us from California, my sister had gone home with Aunt Juanita earlier, but May had stayed with me.

When we were halfway home, I remembered that I had forgotten one of Mother's sitters that I usually took home. I could imagine her waiting for her bus and perhaps missing it, so I turned around and found her walking to the corner.

After letting her out, we came on home. Elsie was at the window overlooking our driveway and called to me to be careful, to shine my lights on the backyard. I did so and then May got out to put the garage door up. The garage was in the basement, and we usually kept the door locked. This time they had unlocked it because they expected me soon.

When they heard a noise, Juanita had called, "Who's down there?" Elsie went to the landing at the back entrance, and just then someone came running up the path through the bushes, but it was too dark for her to see who it was.

Probably someone thought that our visitors would have money on them, and they did, for they foolishly failed to buy travelers checks. What if I had been on time? May might have been knocked down for her purse. Good luck favored us again.

Endearing Memories

I have many endearing memories but will limit the examples to three. This is the most vivid one. The morning after her double mastectomy, my sister came from her room across the hall to see me. She was holding a hemovak in each hand, and I was flat on my back with both hands held down. The love was shining from her big brown eyes as she looked at me. She couldn't reach me for the bed rails, and I couldn't reach her. We were satisfied and happy just to see each other. I hope she could see the love in my eyes, too.

Usually I was more practical—down to earth. I used to scramble eggs for her, and she always said they were so good, nobody could scramble eggs like me. I would always reply, "That's because love is beaten up in them." It was John Ruskin who said, "When Love and Skill work together expect a masterpiece."

Even though this whole book is full of endearing memories, there are several that are especially dear to me, like the two just related. There is another one concerning an incident when Mother was in the hospital in January 1964.

Elsie and I had been reading to her from the devotions in the book, "Climbing the Heights." On this occasion we read one that described a prize winning painting on the subject of Peace, where a seagull was on her nest under a little ledge on the rocky coast, with the wild waves beating against the rocks. Still, the bird was at peace unafraid. So, the author, Keith L. Brooks, implied that we should be at peace in our "believer's retreat" with our faith in God.

Mother said, "This bed is my little nest right now," as she realized that she was being upheld by His "everlasting arms." As we finished I noticed her nurse wiping the tears away. We were moved too.

I thought of this incident later that month when our colored girl, who had helped mother so faithfully for seventeen years, remarked to us in the funeral home, "Your mother's work was done. She had done her duty and is now at peace."

Our faithful friend, Sadie Barber, who had stayed right with us throughout Mother's illness rode with us on the day of the funeral and returned with us to our house afterward. When we saw a vase of deep red roses that had been sent by some of our pupils, I exclaimed, "Oh, I wish Mother could see them!"

Sadie spoke right up and said, "How do you know that she doesn't see them?"

So it is now. I like to feel that Elsie is here watching me. How do I know that she is not?

Being Audited

"Are you her representative?" That was the first question the IRS auditor asked me, as I accompanied my sister into an office in the Federal Building in Charleston.

"Yes," I answered, not knowing that I was anything other than her sister. However, since we did not have a lawyer, I presume that's what he meant.

He was very courteous and motioned us to chairs. Mother had died in January, and this was a hot day in August. Elsie had claimed Mother as a dependent, and the medical expenses were high. We did not have Medicare in those days.

We had had all summer to get ready and had a whole briefcase full of records and receipts. Elsie claimed only 60 percent, because I paid the other 40 percent. Only once did he make me hesitate, when he saw what she had paid.

"Then you claimed the other 40%," he shot at me.

I almost fumbled, before I realized what it meant. Then I replied, "Oh, no, I took the standard deduction."

He was very pleasant as he handed our materials back, saying, "You'll get a refund with interest."

As we passed the girls at their desks on our way out, they all clapped quietly. Although we did not know them, we knew we had friends.

Quiz Shows

My sister and I both taught the same subjects and both sponsored our school papers, so that a description of our teaching days would be about the same. We both had classes in eighth-grade Latin as well as ninth. The 8B semester was divided into two parts that were exploratory, so that pupils could try a subject for nine weeks before deciding what they wanted to choose for an elective. Then we had three full semesters to cover the first-year Latin course. That gave us more time for various projects.

Since derivative work was a part of the course, we used to

clip "It Pays to Increase Your Word Power" from *Reader's Digest*. What a good time we would have had if we had had Peter Funk's book, *High Spirits!* I read it last year and enjoyed the story and also the numerous occasions when the author stops to explain a word with its derivation.

We gained help in teaching from watching or listening to various quiz shows. One game that was good to motivate the youngsters was the "$64.00 Question." We would say, "You could have won $64 if you had been there! *O Tempora! O mores!* How times have changed! Now the proud pupil who could tell the difference between "apiary" and "aviary," because he knew *apis* (bee) and *avis* (bird), could say, "I've won $64,000.00" (not $64.00).

Another time, a contestant could have won a fur coat if she had known what "graminaceous" meant. The class had just had *gramen* (grass) the day before, and some were delighted to make the connection. I always liked to see that look of wonder on the face of the learner when he saw some meaning or solved some problem.

Even after I retired I was always ready to teach my subject. In 1982 when I was in the hospital for hip surgery, a young man in the therapy room was giving me electrical stimulation in my hip and asked me to say some Latin words for him. I did and then told him that he had been using Latin words all his life, like "circus," "plus," minor," "junior," etc. He was amazed when I mentioned the word "preposterous." He knew the meaning of *pre-*and *post-* and saw at once that something can't be "before", and "after" at the same time. So it is absurd—"preposterous." He asked, "Where can I go to get tutored in Latin?" That repaid me for my little bit of teaching. I hope he went on to college as he was planning. He should be successful, for he was ambitious and interested in learning.

More Tornadoes

In 1965 my sister and I drove to the West Coast to visit our aunt in Palm Springs and to attend the wedding of our cousin's son in Eugene, Oregon. We followed that well-known U.S. 66 across the country, although in places we were on I44 under construction. The only trouble was that it rained all the way, and we were surrounded by tornadoes in "Tornado Alley," as it is called.

As we left Springfield, Missouri, one morning we turned on the radio, because we had just read about the bad tornado a few miles south of us during the night, and the announcers were warning us of "funnel clouds." I kept looking in my rearview mirror without saying anything to Elsie about the black, purple sky back of us, but I did step on the gas a little harder. Clouds were on all sides except for one little bright spot far off on the horizon. I said to Elsie, "Look at the map. What direction are we headed?"

She gave me some hope when she answered, "Right toward that bright spot."

Again she turned on the radio to another station, and the first words we heard were "God will take care of you." They were evidently having a morning devotional program.

It is hard to describe the feeling we had, seemingly all alone, on that vast expanse of plains with some mountains in the distance and with that awesome, foreboding sky, and then that "all is well" realization from hearing that reassuring hymn as we spun along the endless miles. We were truly thankful.

When we drove into Kingman, Arizona, at noon the next day, it was bright and clear—storms over. We were so happy to meet our aunt and her friend at the crossroads, for they had come to pilot us along a narrow road north to Hoover Dam. According to the map there wasn't a town for ninety miles. The four of us went into a restaurant for lunch, and we noticed that they were broadcasting a program and interviewing some of the travelers. They did not come to our table, but if they had I would have asked them if they put on a devotional program at breakfast time.

After a delightful visit in Palm Springs we headed north for Oregon, going inland this time, although it was hot. We had lots of road work around Redding but no room for detours. We just had to get through it the best we could. The scenery and the view of Mt. Shasta paid us for driving under difficulties.

After our cousin's wedding we drove south along the beautiful Oregon coast and through groves of redwoods to Eureka, California. At Fortuna we went with our cousin to a rodeo and had a picnic in the woods. The bees wanted my corn on the cob and I had to keep waving it in the air to get the bees off. It's a wonder I didn't get a bee in my mouth. It was fun, anyhow, and we were young (relatively speaking).

When we left Eureka we went north again all the way to Canada. That's where my aunt discovered that she had left her naturalization papers back in the telephone book in Eureka. (She had never married.) Mother became a citizen through marriage. The trip up the Coast was beautiful and easier than it was years before when we had to make time to catch the five ferries on schedule. The only ferry we had this year was at Astoria to cross the Columbia River. We got a picture of the bridge under construction there from our boat.

I didn't get a picture of Mt. Ranier because Elsie was afraid for me to pull off the road or stop, but I did get Lake Coeur d'Alene. We're always inspired by those magnificent mountains in Washington, Idaho, and Montana. We especially enjoyed Snoqualmie Pass. We had storms again in North Dakota and Minnesota, with our radio blaring out, "Get off the road and streets."

We stopped in Morehead City, Minnesota, at a new Holiday Inn partly under construction, where the lady in charge apologized because the T.V. had not been installed or the kitchen completed. All we wanted was a place to sleep. It was a luxurious motel with large plate glass windows separated by a narrow passageway from another plate glass front. That made it safer. Although the wind was only forty miles an hour it was too strong for us, and we were thankful to get in under shelter.

It rained all the way to Duluth and across Wisconsin and Michigan to St. Ignace, where we stayed all night. When we got up the next morning, we started out in the rain, and I made a wrong turn, so that we were headed for Saulte Ste. Marie.

When we came back to the new bridge over the Straits of Mackinac, we could hardly see the floor of the bridge in front of us, let alone the water below. This reminded us of something one of our ministers at home had said in describing the Golden Gate Bridge when it was so foggy you couldn't see either end, but you knew it was "anchored in solid rock on both ends." He made a comparison saying that our lives are anchored in

God's kingdom on either side of this life. Then, I thought, we trust the engineers who build bridges. Why can't we trust God to see us through? Thinking of that hymn again, God did take care of us.

Las Vegas and Gambling

When you hear "Las Vegas," you think of gambling. We thought we would stay way from those places, but the temptation was too great in 1965. My aunt and her friend who met us at Kingman to pilot us down the narrow, crooked steep road through the mountains to Hoover Dam and Lake Mead and then to Las Vegas, prevailed upon us to try our luck.

She knew how we were brought up, so she provided one dollar's worth of nickels for each of us, saying, "Now, it won't hurt you to have a little bit of fun."

Our father was so opposed to gambling he wouldn't buy stock in the company he worked for, when he knew it was good. "No," he said, "What is one man's gain is another man's loss."

We disregarded those teachings for the time being. Elsie put in her first nickel. My, there was such a clatter and noise she thought she had broken the machine and turned around alarmed saying, "What's wrong?"

"Oh," my aunt said, "You've hit the jackpot!"

With that I put in a few nickels in a machine nearby, and the same thing happened, but I knew what it was, having learned from Elsie's experience. She was about to lose all her gains when she hit the jackpot again. Then I did for the second time too. Finally she had $10.00. We both had the same idea—turn it in for a ten-dollar bill; then we won't lose it again. So we went up to the counter with a request to count our money and let us have a bill. So we each tucked a $10 bill down in our purses. I don't know what those cashiers thought. No difference. What has puzzled me up to this day is: how did we happen to win exactly the same amount?

When we got home in Charleston we were feeling a little guilty, so we decided to put the "ill-gotten gains" on the collection plate in our church (without any names). I suppose the people who counted the money after church thought that we must have had visitors in the congregation that Sunday.

This reminded me of another time when we both won the same prize. It wasn't really gambling. Mother was in the hospital, and a nearby florist shop was having their opening. As an inducement they offered gifts to the holders of the winning registration tickets. We went to the shop because we wanted to get flowers for Mother, and naturally we registered our names. That afternoon Elsie got a call that she had won an orchid. Later I got a call saying I had won an orchid. We took them to Mother and she was pleased.

To us merely signing one's name in a store for a chance to win some little prize isn't the same as going to casinos and gambling, especially when we don't have money to throw away. Being teachers we always tried to discourage the idea of "getting something for nothing." We ourselves succeeded fairly well. Even those "sweepstakes" envelopes went into the wastebasket as soon as they came.

P.S.   Alas! My wings had started to sprout but today they are gone. Why? Because I have returned that big "Sweepstakes" envelope saying I might win 10 million dollars. Of course, when I read the fine print, it stipulated $250,000 a year. It would take me forty years to reap the total amount. I might have enough of my own resources to last two years after these new tax laws go into effect, for they will gobble up my little savings fast at the rate they have proposed. Therefore, I must enter all the sweepstakes that come my way.

Police Protection

On our way home from Eureka, California, where we had spent three weeks with our Aunt Elsie, we headed north up the Oregon Coast. We stayed in Newport two nights, because we wanted another little "fling" at hunting agates (not knowing that this year, 1965, would be our last chance to do so).

The second night I was startled by a man speaking to me, as I was trying to find something on the back seat of our car. It was dark and I did not know anyone was near. He said, "I see you're from West Virginia. I'm from there too, only I'm living in New Jersey now. Are you traveling alone?"

"Oh, no!" I said, "We're traveling in two cars, and we keep one another in sight."

"Where are you going?" he inquired next, and when I told him, he said. "You ought to change your plans. Go inland to Rogue River Valley."

I said I had been there and turned to go. I told my sister about him but not my aunt because she always worried about us, as if we were children. The next morning Elsie and I looked at all the license plates but didn't see any from our state or New Jersey. We had not seen any the night before either. We were always curious to see where the other travelers were from.

At Tillamook we stopped at a service station because our windshield had been splashed by a passing truck. Thus we lost sight of my aunt's car. They did not see us stop, and unfortunately, they had made a wrong turn and headed for Portland. We stopped at the cheese factory, where we had planned to meet, but they were not there. We concluded they had gone on, and I tried to catch up with every white car I saw. We knew the way; so we drove on to the Crab Broiler, where we had planned to eat.

After sitting in our parked car about an hour, we went into the restaurant and even called the motel where we had reservations, but no news. Watching for my aunt we kept a close eye on the highway and the parking lot. Before long, an Oregon State Police car came on to the lot, circled our car twice and then parked beside ours. Two officers came in and sat in the booth next to ours.

Finally, Juanita and May arrived, and we were relieved. We were glad also to get a bite to eat. Our aunt was worried when they "lost" us by going on the wrong road, and she had called the state police to request them to watch for us. She would have been worried, if I had told her about the man the night before. When we parked by our cabin at the motor court, a police car was parked there too.

From our court at Seaside we went the next morning to Astoria, and when we came out of the AAA office with our maps, there was a state police car parked behind us. We went into a restaurant, and when we came out, guess what? There was a state police car beside us. I felt like saying "Thank you!"

to those officers, but I was too embarrassed. From Astoria we crossed the Columbia River by ferry over to the state of Washington. We took a picture of the bridge being constructed across the mouth of the river. Even after we got home I still had the impulse to write to the Oregon Police headquarters to express our appreciation, but neglected to do it.

Detours

"The really happy man is the one who enjoys the scenery when he has to take a detour." That quotation was in a booklet of coupons sent to me three years ago by the City of Hope in California. That saying has proved to be true for me, but at the time I was taking some of those detours I did not agree.

One summer we were coming home the northern route and had to take a detour in Idaho. My sister, looking out from her side of the car, exclaimed, "Oh, Ethel, look at the beautiful lake below us!"

Now that lake, Coeur d'Alene, was several hundred feet straight down, and I had no time to look, for I was trying to keep up with the pilot car ahead of me leading us through deep gravel on a detour and I could feel the wheels slipping from side to side in a deep rut. I replied, "We'll be lucky if we don't land in that lake."

I did not see the lake this time but I had once before and also the beautiful Pond Oreille at sunset in the same area. We were on the train and some of our fellow passengers did not even look out the window at the beauty. They were busy playing bridge. I thought to myself—I'll let the engineer do the worrying after this about "getting us there." Elsie was true to that quote. She was enjoying the scenery. She had more confidence in my driving than I had myself, or perhaps she had more faith.

Another time when we were coming home we had a long wait of ninety minutes on a plateau in Wyoming. Again we had a pilot car on a dusty detour, but we had to wait for it to come back for us since we had just missed being included in the first group. The other line coming west did not come through, and everyone wondered what the trouble was. Some travelers got out of their cars and started ballroom dancing on

111

the pavement already finished. All we could do was just sit and watch the jackrabbits. At last we got moving again. The last car carrying the sign in the line before had had a wreck in the deep dust.

In later years when we were not trying to make time on a long trip, we were not dismayed to see the sign "Detour" unless it was a muddy road. We agreed with our aunt who used to say, "Let's take the old road." We knew she was afraid of the freeway, but she also enjoyed the scenery.

We too appreciated the chance to go on country roads. In West Virginia we had a song entitled "Country Roads," which everyone liked. On an interstate about all the driver can see is cars coming toward him and, looking in his rearview mirror, cars following him. I like to see the cows coming in to be milked or sheep gamboling across the field.

I hope I haven't taken the reader on too many figurative detours, but I do have a habit of making comments. Few people have a real emergency, when speed is necessary, whether it's on a road or reading a book. Just as I like to enjoy the road scenery, so I like to take time to enjoy the writer's word pictures. Perhaps he has described a place where we have been or has told about a situation that was similar to one we had experienced. In our day in journalism class we had to stick to the facts only without any adjectives. Now some papers are allowing more embellishment especially in the features.

Alpha Delta Kappa

In 1968 the Alpha Chapter of Alpha Delta Kappa in West Virginia voted us into this international sorority for women educators. We had a beautiful initiation program at the home of Maryida Mosby, an outstanding teacher of civics. There were five of us to be initiated and we were really thrilled with the candlelight service.

We were able to attend all the meetings for the next two years and benefited from their programs aimed at making us more inspiring teachers. In 1969 we went to the international convention in Kansas City, Missouri.

There were twenty sisters besides the husband of one member and the driver on our own special bus. I always carried my black carry-all every time we got off. Finally one member said, "Why don't you leave that bag on the bus? It's safe enough."

What we didn't tell her or anyone else was that the bag had boxes of our "rocks" that we had been polishing and setting in jewelry. We were planning to put them on the exhibit table for Arts and Crafts and were keeping it a secret. They were rather heavy.

There was one rather amusing incident that happened in Kansas City. It shows the advantage of being a twin. Of course, we know that you can't be in two places at one time, but we did the next best thing.

When the bus driver stopped on the corner near the front of the Muehlebach Hotel, our headquarters, he put all the baggage out on the sidewalk, although five of us had been assigned to rooms in the Aladdin Hotel next door. The driver couldn't take us to the entrance, because it was on a one-way street. Elsie walked down to the lobby in our hotel and asked the clerk if he could send a bellboy up to the corner to get our luggage.

He asked, "How will he know it's your luggage?"

Elsie said, "My twin sister is guarding it. She looks just like me." The people around all laughed. With that the bellhop left and found me without any trouble.

Another member of our party, noting our lights bags said, "Let me carry one of your bags," and picked it up. "He can carry this heavy one of mine." I gave the boy a tip, and my sister laughed with me about it.

We thoroughly enjoyed our week. To note the highlights, Elsie and I wrote a poem about it after we came home and gave everyone a copy. (I had been taking notes all the way.) At one of our meetings we also showed slides we had taken.

Let Me Come Back

"Let Me Come Back" was the name of a play that I ordered from the National Education Association to use in my homeroom guidance class. When it came we were all surprised to see that the place where the play took place was in room 207 in a high school. That was the number of my room. The name of the teacher in the cast was Miss Jones. What a coincidence!

The pupils enjoyed giving it, for it was timely, since this was during World War II. The main character was a pilot of a bomber flying in the dark over enemy territory, and he had only his own thoughts to keep him company and awake. He recalls a line from a poem by Keats, that had been assigned to his class to learn, beginning: "A thing of beauty is a joy forever."

He wants to go back to tell his teacher, Miss Jones, about it and to urge her pupils to learn their memory passages. He was glad he knew the lines, although he had not wanted to learn them at the time. Now he wants to thank her. His ghost comes into the schoolroom to accomplish his purpose.

Isn't it a good thing to memorize Bible verses or poems and hymns, so that when we are alone in the dark, perhaps lying on a hospital bed, we can take solace in repeating them to ourselves!

All through my sister's teaching career, her schedule was like mine, except that she had more classes in English and, therefore, more opportunity to teach beautiful poetry. She sponsored a poetry club, and one evening, I remember, Mother had invited the members to a party at our house; she gave each one a copy of *One Hundred and One Famous Poems.*

A passage that we both enjoyed teaching was the one beginning, "And what is so rare as a day in June?" from Lowell's "The Vision of Sir Launfal." We had learned part of that poem in high school in our junior year, and we were both grateful to our teacher, Miss Anna Dunn. She had quotations on her board every day for us to learn, and we memorized poetry too. I don't think the month of June ever passed after that without one of us saying to the other, "What is so rare as a day in June?" and then going on with the rest of it as far as either of us could remember it.

Hurdles

Perhaps the best way to summarize the forty-three years I spent teaching would be to review the hurdles met (but not always conquered). We may save the bigger hurdles, like the first day I taught, for separate coverage. At the end of my career, I wrote a little farewell message for the school paper, from which I may quote later.

Since it was near the end of the term, and we were having track meets, I thought about hurdles and wrote a story that got lost. Two paragraphs are given here because they are applicable, not only to my teaching but to all teaching.

"Life is full of hurdles, some high and some low, but a teacher's life is just one hurdle after another in the race to come out at the end of the year with the victory won. What victory?

"Victory over ignorance, greed, intolerance and all the rest. From the first day of the term to the last we are racing, and many are the obstacles set in our path to make victory a little harder. 'The greater the obstacle the more glory in overcoming it.' Moliere said."

That is a quotation I often had on my blackboard, but it was meant for my pupils, not for me. Certain challenges, like meeting five classes a day and bringing them out at the end of the year beaming with knowledge and good will, we expect and we meet such hurdles with determination like a housewife attacking a stack of dishes to be washed.

For me, getting a school paper out every two weeks was a constant and continuing hurdle. However, we anticipated that. It was the extra, unexpected hurdles that kept me in a turmoil. My highest hurdle was an assembly program. Even on the first day of school, while the principal was welcoming us all back and reading the opening bulletin to us, I was surreptiously leafing through the bulletin to see if my name was listed in the assembly schedule. Horrors! It was! My name always appeared. What is there to celebrate in January?

From then on, I had to hurry to find suitable material in order to forestall the youngsters bringing in some play like "Shooting Grandma." (Any similarity in title to an existing play is purely coincidental.) The really big assembly I had to plan was the honor society induction. You would have thought this induction service would have excused me from other assembly programs. Evidently the principal did not think so.

There were a few low hurdles, like P.T.A. meetings, but the first one of those for the year would qualify for a "big high jump," for that was when the parents came out in force to follow the children's schedule for fifteen-minute periods. To me that time seemed longer than the forty-five minute classes we had daily with the children. Another thing, since most of the children had two parents we sometimes had a hard time finding seats for them all. I was never a public speaker, but I didn't have the nerve that one of our teachers had when she told them, "We'll just have study hall."

Visitors' Day, familiar to most teachers, was stretched out to Visitors' Week in our school, and no matter how long one had taught, it still put "butterflies in your stomach." Children are so unpredictable.

The Christmas programs were really a pleasure, for I could let my pupils sing carols in Latin and not be limited to "Santa Claus Is Coming to Town." I had the words for "Rudolph the Red-Nosed Reindeer" in Latin and they sang it too with gusto. One of my pupils always had to lead the singing.

Another hurdle I enjoyed was preparing for the annual exhibits of our class work, not only in our own building but in the Civic Center for all the secondary schools in the county. All year long the children had been bringing in work, often astounding me.

Two girls did surprise me by bringing in a Roman house they had made by looking at pictures they had found in a reference book. It was three feet long, just the right size to fit on a table in the room. They omitted a roof, so that we could look down into it and see all the furniture they had made and the dolls dressed like Romans.

My sister had a similar project with characters from the Trojan War dressed like Greeks standing by some Greek columns. One that attracted the most attention was a ceramic Trojan horse about eight inches high on a platform with rollers under it. Tiny soldiers were descending from the door in the side of the horse. The girl who made it was fortunate, because her family had a kiln at home.

Most of the projects, however, were posters showing how "Latin Lives Today" and were based upon derivatives of Latin used in law, medicine, science, etc. Always there were some model ships or Roman chariots, which they enjoyed making.

Although the induction of new members into the National Junior Honor Society was a big hurdle it was gratifying to me. We followed a point system in order to avoid any discontent about why some pupil did not make it. Nevertheless it took time to count all those points and keep it secret. At first we had real candles on the table and in the hands of the inductees for the service, but one day a girl with long hair came up to the table to get her certificate and I noticed her hair on the side next to me smoking. I batted it out with my hand as quickly as I could and whispered to her to keep her candle away from her face. After that we used electrified candles on the table and small flashlights for the new members. It really was an inspiring program, beginning with "I would Be True" by the Glee Club and with "Follow the Gleam" at the close.

At the end of the year we had Orientation Day for the sixth graders who would be entering our school in the fall. For me this was a hurdle, because we had to make preparation for them. Since I took pictures for our paper, it fell to me, some-how, to take slides for a program depicting life in junior high with all its activities, from sports to music and in various rooms like home economics, woodworking, art, library, etc. I hope they didn't get the idea it was all play.

I have already mentioned getting the school paper out on time every two weeks but having my staff like a class every day helped. When the printer brought the copies we had to deliver them to the rooms and send out the exchanges For me, there was actual work in climbing three flights of stairs to get to the engravers, where I handed in the pictures we had taken to get cuts made and mounted on wood, type high. Getting the films to the camera shop and then going after the pictures consumed time. My Saturday mornings were devoted to these errands. I got my sister into the act by letting her run into the store, while I sat at the wheel, in case I had to double park.

Graduation brought more hurdles, too numerous to men-tion, with Class Day, parties, awards assembly, and student speakers for commencement to be coached. I remember staying late one night after the program hunting a robe that was missing. We had had the graduates assemble in the big study hall to get their robes before taking their places in line. There were old-fashioned seats and desks in that room, and sure enough, one of the graduates had stuffed his robe into a desk. We finally thought of looking there.

Also near the end of the term came the achievement tests,

a hurdle for me, if not for the pupils. I did not worry too much about the I.Q. tests, for I felt in no way responsible. Nevertheless I felt bad if the scores were low. It was a different story with achievement tests, because I was always afraid some one would actually show a regression.

Now we were entitled to a good vacation and rest. But no! We went to summer school some years, and then we were taking tests instead of giving them. After retirement I was asked, "Would you do it again?"

"Gladly! Yes, I would," I usually answered, "Provided I had my youth back with some agility as well as good mobility." I have heard of people teaching from a wheelchair, but I surely wouldn't want to try it, not with conditions the way they are today.

Now that we had come to the finish line, let me assure you that, although we may not have won first prize, we enjoyed the race, in spite of, no, perhaps because of the obstacles. That quotation from Moliere was meant for me after all. We felt the flush of excitemet and got more satisfaction from jumping hurdles than from standing still.

"Palma non sine pulvere!"
(No prize without the dust of conflict!)

Reminiscences Upon Retiring

In this chapter I shall try to summarize my teaching experiences or else give a few quotes from the story that I had in our school paper when I retired in 1969. The first day was a hectic one, so I shall quote to show how I felt.

"To most of you forty-three years seems like a long time, but to me it seems like only yesterday that I eagerly and somewhat apprehensively made my way to Lincoln Junior High School, where I had been assigned to teach. In those days we did not get our schedules ahead of time (At least I didn't.) So that first morning when I was handed mine, I was dismayed because mine had vocational guidance, civics, history—subjects I had not prepared to teach."

(This was not printed in the *Lincoln Log* story, but I found out later that one teacher had requested these subjects and also problem children. The trouble was she did not show up when school started so I fell heir to her schedule for that semester, since I was the newest teacher there.) "But I had no time to worry or to prepare, for in a few minutes there came bounding into my room a whole flock of beaming, excited, talkative youngsters, and every forty-five minutes a new flock came, until we came to the end of the day, and I was in a daze. Probably I was dazed all year. I learned more history than ever before. I hope the pupils learned some too. Speaking of in-service (teacher work-days) we had it; only we received no pay for it. Once a week I went after school to take penmanship lessons in order to earn a Palmer certificate. They didn't tell us at the university that we had to learn to write. We typed. Yes, I taught penmanship in homeroom. I always gave some dependable boy the job of passing out the bottles of ink, and someone else passed out the penholders and points. I made ovals on the board for the class to imitate and sang (?) a rhythmic 'Push, Pull' as I demonstrated making lines using the arm muscles."

(Today I am glad I learned this myself, for arthritis has crippled my fingers so that I depend on muscular motion.)

"At our first faculty meeting the principal instructed us on what to do if the supervisor or superintendent came in. We were to have the pupils rise and say, "Good morning, Dr.———" or "Good afternoon Miss B———," I was always afraid they would not understand who the visitor was.

Once I expressed the hope that television would not invade our classrooms before I retired, because I am not photogenic. I did not know at the time that I was being prophetic, if not photogenic. We had already had one meeting to learn all about I.T.T. (instructional television) planned for next year. I seem to have hit the nail on the head, for in June I shall retire.

What am I looking forward to most? Frankly, not having to get up at 5:30, and in winter, not looking out the window to see if it had snowed during the night, making it hard for me to take my car off the hill.

What shall I miss most? All the cheery greetings, "Hello, Miss Jones!" called out half a dozen times within ten minutes, if I happened to meet the same person half a dozen times in the hall. Again, I shall miss the chorus of "goodbyes." I must admit, though, I was happy to say goodbye sometimes and send the youngsters home to their mothers. I suppose I'll miss the teasing and tricks too. If these teenagers could just have been as clever in answering their test questions as in making smart remarks, they would all have made A. For example, some one would say, "You are the best Latin teacher," and then after a pause, "in the building," when they knew that I was the only Latin teacher in the building.

"Really, I have enjoyed most of the time spent here. Like the sundial, I'll record, or remember, only the sunny hours. I have taught many of the parents of my present pupils, and just recently a boy told me that I had had his grandmother in school. So I guess it is time for me to say thanks and farewell. *Valete!*"

The school paper, *The Lincoln Log,* came out the last week of school, and although the pupils all had copies of it, they asked me in each class to read my story to them.

Teaching Full of Adventure

I would consider our whole teaching career an adventure. Someone might say, "How could you have any adventures in a routine school day, teaching the same subject in the same place for forty-three years?"

True, but the children changed and each child was different. That made it interesting. One never knows what to expect from youngsters. In the war years we used to hear the song, "Praise the Lord and Pass the Ammunition."

The schools were crowded, and we could say that we did our best to teach the children and then passed them along to the next grade. It would be monotonous in a factory, where all the products coming off the line were from the same die or cast. Not so with children!

They have robots in some factories working like people, for example, assembling cars. Now I hope you young people preparing for your life work will take note. We will always need teachers. No robot could take the place of a teacher's guiding hand helping a child, just as nothing can replace a mother's loving care.

"I wonder whether there is in America a statue just to a classroom teacher." This sentence caught my eye in an article by George H. Henry in an educational magazine that I was reading some time ago, and I copied it down, for it was a challenge to me. It stood out like a bright star blinking for consideration. The author did not have the answer, and neither do I.

I do know what the author means, and I appreciate his implied tribute to the teacher. Although there may not be a statue in marble or bronze, there are thousands of living memorials, and we teachers need no other. No greater reward is needed than the realization that one has contributed in a small measure to a worthy life. We are justified, I believe, in asserting that successful men and women are memorials, not only to their parents but to their teachers as well.

Thirty Years Too Soon?

Were we "born thirty years too soon?" That is the question! My sister once wrote a paper on that subject for our creative writing group here at the Village and concluded that we did well to come into this world when we did. For one thing they had not started having those noisy flashing-light programs in the disco joints that would ruin your eyes, dull your hearing, and "drive you up the wall."

We as retired teachers can't help feeling a little gleeful that we didn't have some of the problems that they have today. We had no drugs (at least, that we knew about). There were no areas marked off "for smoking for students." In fact another teacher and I one summer had charge of the civil service exams given in a school building where it was strictly against the law to smoke in a school. Consequently we were considered "old meanies" by the men who wanted to smoke when we said, "no."

We did not have windowless all-purpose rooms with no divisions between classes. We liked our own little bailiwick and also enjoyed being able to look out the window. As for me, I looked out often in winter to see if it was snowing; if so I might not be able to get my car up the hill. The worst thing we had to contend with was an occasional paper wad (or "spitball").

This commentary is not a matter of "sour grapes." We really did enjoy our teaching and seeing that look of wonder on the faces of our pupils when they learned something.

We appreciated the slower pace—such as travel by train, when we had time to look out the window at the passing scenes. We had no fear of hijacking or of falling through space.

We were happy, even though we did not have many of the modern conveniences of this jet age. We sincerely wish the younger generation the best of everything. We admire their skill in using computers and we know there will be more inventions for their use, Good luck to them all.

A Close Call

On the day before Thanksgiving in 1969, when were visiting our aunt in Palm Springs, California, we went to see the Wonderland of Rocks and had to drive seven miles over a rough, deserted road to get to a certain point, where, on a clear day, you could see ninety miles to the Imperial Valley.

We got there, turned the engine off, walked to the lookout point and admired the view. I was glad when we started home, for I never did like deserted places, and we had seen no other people. All we saw was a coyote at the edge of the road and he darted away.

The next day we had reservations for Thanksgiving dinner at a hotel. When we got into the car, much to our dismay, it would not start. My aunt called the AAA station, which fortunately was located near the hotel, and it was open. So help came. The battery was "dead," and water on the cement below showed it had burst. While we were eating, a new battery was installed.

Wasn't that luck or was it something more than that? What if that had happened in that lonely place the day before?

Earthquakes

We were lucky also when it came to earthquakes. In 1969 when we were visiting our aunt again in Palm Springs during the Christmas season, we heard a loud thump one morning early and thought a truck had hit the house. Just then my aunt came running in saying, "Don't get alarmed, girls; it's just a little earthquake!"

We got dressed, ready to run out if we had to. The houses

there are low on that account—mostly just one story. I thought about Mt. San Jacinto towering 8000 feet above us. We could see it through the long picture window the whole length of our aunt's front room. We used to watch the incline cars on the tramway going up and down and passing at midpoint as they carried sightseers to the top.

We did not go up. For one thing, we did not have a clear day while there, so we had a good excuse. I thought about those rocks that might come tumbling down. In 1965 we had driven up that steep road to the landing station. I had wanted to test the brakes on our new car because I had inadvertently left them on while we drove two miles to an ice cream parlor for date milk shakes. (By the way, the date bits won't come through the straw. Don't try it.)

The story goes that even Governor Brown stood in the middle of the car and would not look down. I bought a set of slides on the tramway and that satisfied us.

One other time we came near being in an earthquake. It happened the day before we arrived in Arcata in June 1932. We had read about it in the Portland paper and worried, because the story said it was worse than the 1906 quake as far as their area was concerned. One woman was killed by a falling chimney. All the medicines in the drugstores plunged to the floor making a great mess. Our aunt took us around to see the damage.

As to sandstorms, we just experienced one, and that was in Palm Springs one Sunday morning. We decided we would go to church, although our aunt warned us we might not have any paint left on our car. We wanted to go. When we were taking pictures of the church that week, the minister had come out and had given us some postcard views of it—a beautiful building.

The wind was blowing but not as strong as it did a little later. Even with the windows of the car wound up tight, I could feel the gritty sand between my teeth, and when we got to the church, we had to hold our hats and run as fast as we could to the building for shelter. A few other people were out. After this I'll pay attention to the people who live in a place for any precautions necessary.

Our Last Trip by Train

In November 1969 we took our last trip by train. Our aunt who lived in Palm Springs, wanted us to see California in winter, especially at Christmas. Since we were retired, we were able to go. We decided to travel on the train, I think, from nostalgia for bygone days. We had not been on a train since 1958. To tell the truth, we were timid about flying. We were also concerned about the threatened railroad strikes and the unrest in the Bay area around Berkeley.

We were planning to leave on the George Washingon at 2:00 A.M. and that caused us a little worry too. As it turned out later we were justified in that misgiving, because the ticket agent in that station was murdered by robbers late one night.

Also, we remembered that our father had been saved years before in a similar situation, late at night in a deserted railroad station. Two rough looking men came in, and one whispered to the other, "There's your man over there," nodding toward Father. He caught that whisper. Just then a train an hour late pulled into the station Father did not know where it was going, but he jumped up and got on it, not waiting for his train to come. That was luck!

Since our retirement in June we had been busy with volunteer work and going to our sorority convention in Kansas City, so that we did not have time to grieve over not going back to the classroom. We were especially happy about that, for on the very morning that we had bought our tickets and were returning home we found our way blocked by students from the nearby high school. They were running and yelling in the streets. The unrest among the young people had reached a peak, culminating in what they liked to call a "riot." I had had a few wishful thinkers the year before, telling me, "There's going to be a riot, Miss Jones." I did not pay too much attention to it then.

I wanted to drive into our garage but there was a gang coming up the hill toward us. Elsie got out of the car and held up her hand, saying, "Let her into our garage." They stopped, thank goodness, and we stayed in the rest of the day, packing and listening to the radio. The pupils in the junior highs in our area were not allowed to change classes that day but just stayed where they were the second period with whoever their teacher happened to be. I did not envy those teachers.

The next morning at 2 A.M. we left the house in a downpour of rain for the C & O station. We were relieved to find three other travelers in the waiting room. When the conductor collected our tickets he said, "You are in for a few surprises." Indeed we did notice some changes. There were no redcaps. the beautiful new station in Cincinnati was deserted. The train we boarded for Chicago had one passenger coach, and we even waited on a siding somewhere for a freight to go through.

In Chicago our tickets were taken in the station, and no one challenged our occupancy of our bedroom after the porter put us on the Super Chief. We just told him where we belonged.

We had a wonderful time in Palm Springs with our aunt and took many trips—to Disneyland, Oceanside, Los Angeles, and elsewhere. In January we came back on the Super Chief to Chicago. After the balmy weather in southern California we nearly froze. It was five below zero the day we arrrived in Chicago and the wind chill factor made it 40 below. We finally got a taxi to our hotel, where they gave us a room that would accommodate eight. We left so early the next morning the coffee shop wasn't open; we got along on a glass of hot water.

Our tracks coming East along the lake were frozen and had to be thawed. When we went to the diner we slid all around on the platforms and had to hold on to the icy door handles with gloved hands. In Toledo we had to wait three hours for our train south because they had to thaw the switches so our train from the north could get through. When it did come, my sister and I as well as three other passengers were watching for it from an upstairs window in the hall. We rushed to the head of the stairs, and the trainmen down below called up, "How many are there of you?"

I answered, "Five."

"Come on!" he said.

The pipes on that train too were frozen, so there was no coffee. However we did get a toasted sandwich. (I don't know whether they had microwave then or not, but I watched them put it, already in a bag, in the oven.) It didn't take long. When I took it to Elsie, she said, "That's the best thing I ever tasted!"

When we arrived in Charleston at 1:30 A.M. we were worried about getting a taxi. As we were coming down the steps, we heard familiar voices saying, "There they are!"

What a good surprise! Our friend and neighbor, Beulah Blessing, and her brother Leslie had come to meet us in that terrible cold weather with the streets all ice. Other neighbors had turned on our furnace, had the light on it the house, and had breakfast on the table, with other goodies, like cookies and fruit cake, stored away for us. We were very grateful for that warm (entirely unexpected) welcome home. That's the way it was on all our trips and even at home; we owed so much to so many people that we felt forever indebted because we could not begin to return their kindnesses.

(Postlude) I picked up our local paper recently and saw an article with the dateline, Charleston, W. Va. It was the picture that caught my eye, for it showed the Chessie Cat painted on the front of an engine of the CSX system (formerly C & 0). That brought back memories of our train trips, because our baggage bore the familiar picture of a cat asleep with one paw tucked under her chin. The envelopes containing our tickets also had that picture with the slogan "sleep like a kitten." I still have one piece of luggage with the Chessie Cat picture on it. It did make me rather sad to read that this logo will not be used any more on the trains, engines, or sides of cars.

An Encouraging Incident

In connection with the so-called "riot" mentioned in that story on the last train trip, I'd like to relate an incident that encouraged me and sheds a little more light on the young people of that restless period.

In 1968 during the regular class periods of the last day before the Christmas vacation, a time when youngsters ordinarily are their noisiest, we had a program beginning on a serious note with some carols sung in Latin and a few poems. Then I read "The Star Still Shines," an excerpt from a sermon by Dr. Curtis K. Jones, pastor of our church, which was addressed to the young people, indicating how they can make their lives count for good and keep the light shining, as part of the light is entrusted to them. We concluded with the well-known quotation, "I am only one, but I am one!"

The whole class stood up by their seats and then quietly sat down again. One of them asked, "Was he related to you, Miss Jones?"

I answered, "No," but I would have been very proud if I could have said "Yes." They must have told the other classes, for each one that day stood, not in tribute to me but to the writer of that sermon.

That sermon had been delivered by Dr. Jones in our church in 1948, and I had read excerpts from it before without incident. This year I had not expected their reaction, and it made me very happy for it renewed my faith in our young people. What was true in 1968 in my class is true today too, for everywhere young people on the whole are idealistic and respond to appeals to their natural altruistic desire to help others.

I could recount many examples of this. I see it in the dining room in this retirement facility where I live. The waitresses are eager to please everyone. So are the cleaning girls that come every two weeks. In our medical center the nurses are also solicitous in taking care of the elderly patients. The girls who come to help me are an inspiration to all of us.

In the hospital where my sister was a terminal patient, everyone showed TLC, that "tender loving care" we read about. My sister realized that God was sending love to her in the person of those tending her. She asked me to hunt up an agate that she herself had found, polished, and set in a key ring, so that she could give each nurse a little souvenir, "something to remember me by."

PART IV
AFTER RETIREMENT

Volunteers

"This is my lucky day!" That was the way our director of volunteers at the Charleston General Hospital greeted us when we went to be interviewed. It was a lucky day for us, too, because we felt so let down, not having to return to the class-room when school opened.

Without having time to ask questions, we found ourselves in pink uniforms heading for the information desk and the glass-enclosed gift shop next to it. Elsie recalled making one mistake. She directed a doctor who asked for medical records to the medical library in another building.

I probably did some things wrong too but did not realize it. I was glad we just had an old-fashioned money drawer and not a new cash register that I didn't know how to operate. Elsie had her problem with a whole row of phones and push buttons, to transfer calls and put on "hold." School teachers and no experience with such things.

Anyway, I tried to sell a few things but spent most of my time entertaining the little folks who came rushing in to see the stuffed animals. I let them pick them up, and they had a good time while waiting to see the doctor. This happened to be crippled children's day and their parents out in the lobby could watch them through the glass partition. One little girl, I remember, took the same stuffed skunk out each week to show to her mother. In the middle of the morning two other volunteers brought the refreshment cart around and gave each child a bag containing a lunch, usually a sandwich and a carton of milk.

Elsie was interested in watching a little fellow running in where I was and then out. He finally asked her a question and immediately went running to his mother, yelling, "Yes, Mama, they are twins!" That caused a ripple of laughter, and all eyes turned toward us.

We really did enjoy our work there. We did a variety of things—filing, typing, working on their news bulletin, delivering flowers and helping in the therapy rooms. Sometimes on Sunday we were responsible for meeting the minister who was coming to give the message in chapel. We took patients to the service, passed out hymn books, and locked up afterwards.

One Sunday I was pleased to hear a little crippled boy in a wheelchair speak up, when the minister had finished, and say, "Thank you for praying for me." His parents were not there. They lived out in the country.

On Radio

We never expected to be on radio but it came as a surprise, not giving us time to refuse. Early one Sunday morning in February 1971, I brought in our paper, and there we were on page 1 of Section E (in our volunteer uniforms in the accompanying picture). Elsie was holding Raggedy Andy and I was holding Raggedy Ann in the gift shop of the hospital where we had been working since July 1969. We knew our pictures had been taken but did not know the Volunteer Council in the County had voted us runners—up in the Volunteer of the Year Competition.

The top place was won by a chemist from Carbide who did tutorial work (something new that year) with pupils who needed help in math. The story of our work and the pictures covered the whole front page of the section. The manager of the shop had been in New York and was surprised when she returned on Monday. She tacked the whole page on the door entering the shop. Then she made arrangements for us to go to a radio studio for a half hour interview on March 16 at noon.

On that day we went to the WTIP studio, accompanied by

our manager. We did not have a rehearsal—just talked as Shirley Annod, announcer, asked us questions. It helped me because Shirley had been one of my pupils years before. We had not told anyone ahead of time, and some of our friends asked, "Why didn't you tell us? We would have listened." That was just it. We had not wanted anyone to hear us in case we made a mistake. However, some friends did hear it because they always listened to the radio at the noon hour. The director of volunteers, who had sent our names in, and her assistant in our hospital had listened and assured us that we "did fine." I'm glad it wasn't T.V. I would have been scared.

Retired Teachers Group

As soon as we retired, we joined the NRTA and the local as well as state organizations. Almost immediately we had a job to do. Since we typed, they asked us to keep the membership lists with all the addresses and telephone numbers. With over 1200 retired school employees in the county, you can imagine what a job that was. We did have helpers—fifty telephone callers.

We had to call the callers, however, before each meeting, although programs had been sent out at the beginning of the school year. At first, we thought that would mean just once a month. But no, during the legislative sessions, we had to call those committees. Also it meant hunting through the telephone book to verify numbers and making changes in addresses—a never-ending job.

My sister and I used to take registration at a desk near the door of the room where we met and gave out name tags. One day, when we were not able to do this on account of our disabling arthritis but were still able to notify the callers, a woman that I called asked me, "Whatever happened to those twins that used to stand by the door? We used to watch them."

I told her I was one of them and explained why we did not come any more. (We did not know we were on exhibit.)

Publicity for My Hand

In 1977 my right hand got publicity and pictures in a national magazine, but I didn't. Nobody knew whose hand it was.

It happened this way. I had been taking gold shots for my rheumatoid arthritis since 1972. My sister had been taking shots since 1970, and her arthritis was getting better. One day she saw our doctor in the drugstore and told him. "My arthritis is getting better, but now my sister has it."

"That's right," he said, "When you want to get rid of something just give it to someone else."

In 1976 a rheumatologist had said to me, "If you don't want to spend the rest of your life in a wheelchair, you'll have to have that right knee joint replaced. Shall I call the hospital now?"

I hesitated, "Let me consult my sister in the waiting room."

"No, make up your mind," he insisted and so his secretary called to make arrangements with a surgeon. My sister was surprised when I told her, for we had always consulted one another.

After the knee surgery I got along very well until the next year when my hand got bad. As one doctor said "It comes and goes."

I said, "I wish it would just go!"

A specialist in hand surgery was called in, and preparatory to operating, he put in a shot of a cortisone derivative. That did it! Saturday night that right hand was so swollen it looked like a baseball mitt, and the doctor was out of town. Sunday at 2:00 A.M. a big nodule near the pulse on my wrist burst, and my sister had a time with alcohol swabs taking care of it.

Tuesday the orthopedist was back in his office, and I was his first patient. Alarmed, he asked, "Has Dr. S—seen this?"

"No," I said, "You're my doctor." Then I asked, "Does it have gangrene in it?" I did not like that yellow, red, green, and black discoloration.

"Not yet!" he replied.

That wasn't very encouraging. Anyhow he managed to get a room in the hospital after insisting, "It's an emergency!"

For six weeks I stayed there with the left arm held down by IV's and the right arm in hot packs! My sister was there every day to feed me, but she needed attention too. Since I was already taken care of, I persuaded her to have that biopsy that should have been done a year earlier, but the mammograms had been negative and fooled the doctors.

She was in surgery from 7:00 A.M. to 7 P.M. for double mastectomies. It was the longest day I ever spent. When she was brought back to her room across the hall from me, first one friend and then another went in to see her. I couldn't stand it any longer, so I told the nurse, "Get a wheelchair and take me over there." When I got to the door, the first thing Elsie said was, "Who fed you today?"

She went home in three weeks but I was still there. Finally word came from the Disease Center in Atlanta to put me on TB medicine. They did and the trouble started to clear up at once. The cortisone had reactivated the TB, as we all knew it could. One doctor said, "It's easier to cure TB than arthritis." Nothing was easy for me, especially getting seven cultures out of my hand by a suction machine on the wall.

Now, to get to the pictures. A team of specialists from our state university and a photographer had come from Morgantown to see my hand and take pictures. I did not see the medical journal they were in, but the next year when I was in the hospital for my turn with mastectomies they took pictures again, to show "Before" and "After."

Later I met a friend, a doctor in our church. He was in charge of the WVU programs in our local hospital, and when I told him about it, he said, "I saw those pictures but didn't know it was your hand." Even after we came to Carolina Village, when I was giving our new doctor my medical history and mentioned it, he said, "Oh, yes, I saw your hand in that magazine."

Our of the Hospital

We were both so happy to be home again. For a month I had a nurse, a lovely young R.N., a newlywed, an accomplished organist and pianist. As soon as she came in she announced, "You are my first patient!" Oh, but she was careful in counting out those pills. One prescription had said, "Fatal if more than three are taken." So she kept looking at her chart. When she wasn't busy with my hot packs, she played the piano for us.

Elsie had a visiting nurse that the doctors had sent. One of our good neighbors, Mrs. Newcomer, who had taken us to the doctors and elsewhere in her car, contacted another neighbor, whom we had never met, and she volunteered to work for us. We paid her, of course, and also paid for our meals delivered by Meals on Wheels. Those volunteers were lovely people, and we made many new friends. One gentlemen even brought roses several times. Our housekeeper had a hard time trying to clean the living room, for she said it was like "Grand Central Station."

Another Example of Serendipity

When I think back over the past, I can recall many serendipitous events. Finding out about Carolina Village was one. We were both in the hospital at the same time in 1977. Our only relatives were three cousins, children of our only first cousin (deceased), living in California.

When our minister asked, "What your going to do now? Are you going into a nursing home?" we did not have an answer. Then we told a friend and she surprised us by saying that she had visited eighteen retirement homes in this country and liked Carolina Village, where she is now, the best. So we got on the waiting list and moved in without ever coming to see it.

Elsie called our cousins in California to tell them of our plans to move, and David Thomson, the cousin in the Air Force, said he, his wife and his father would come to help us. However, they were "bumped" from their flight and did not arrive until the morning the moving van left Charleston.

Because there was construction on the West Virginia Turnpike we decided to go west to Lexington, Kentucky, and then south and east to Hendersonville. We were very thankful to David for driving us in our car, and although I offered to drive, he said, "You just enjoy the scenery." That is just what all of us did, for it is a beautiful drive on interstates all the way through forests and mountains.

Moving In

On Memorial Day 1980 we were resting in our motor court when a call came from Carolina Village. "Your moving people are here at the back entrance near your apartment with their van," the girl on the phone said.

"We'll be right over," Elsie said, and then we had to hurry. We had been told that since Monday was a holiday, they would arrive Tuesday. It was a disadvantage because there were no maintenance men here to help. Our cousins had come by plane from California to help us and drive us here in our car. Elsie showed them where to put things.

I couldn't help any, so I sat down in a big overstuffed chair in our lounge. I talked with some of our residents. When I got up to come over to see how things were progressing, I looked down at my hands and arms. They were black as coal. My dress was black; I looked like a coal miner. That fire that had occurred in the Village prior to our arrival had put soot on everything.

Our nearest neighbors were Mr. and Mrs. Oliphant, and they told us all about the fire ten days before. It was in our hall and the smoke rolling down was so dense they had had to wrap their faces in wet towels and feel with their hands for the wall to get to the back door, which was only six feet from their doorway. Most of the residents on the first floor were pulled through the windows by firemen. As soon as I got a chance I got my yardstick out and measured that window in our bedroom. It was only 14 inches wide. "I'll have to reduce," I said.

A New Life

"To have joy one must share it;
happiness was born a twin."

That is the quotation that I used at the beginning of an article that I wrote for our creative writing group shortly after coming to Caroline Village Retirement Complex in 1980. This old Indian saying was on a Christmas card that a resident,

Mrs. Margaret Leonard, had sent us and it inspired me to make some comments on our new life in the Village. I let Mrs. Leonard read it, and she took it to the editor of *The Villager,* our paper. That's how it happened to be published under the title "My Twin and I."

I'll give you a few excerpts to show how we felt about our new home:

"This Indian quote is typical of our being together—not only in opening Christmas packages but in all our experiences— our pleasures, and yes, even our sorrows. It has made our joys double and our griefs or worries divided.

Is it any wonder that we felt like Alice in Wonderland (two Alices) when we wandered through the halls hand in hand in Carolina Village marveling at the many evidences of talent displayed by our residents, from paintings hanging on the walls to crafts in the showcase?

No matter how many good features we found, they woudl mean little without the friendliness of the people who made us feel welcome, that we were part of one big happy family. Yes, we had many things for which to be thankful. In fact, we wake up every morning saying to one another,

'This is the day the Lord hath made,

Let us rejoice and be glad in it!'"

Note: the quote at the beginning of this chapter was true for our whole lives together and really sets the tone for this book.

Post Scriptum

Perhaps you would be interested in knowing what the card was like that had this quotation on it. It shows two small, brown bears, one standing at the roadside mail box pulling out packages with Christmas ribbons on them and passing them down to the other bear seated on the ground opening them. Written in ink beside one bear was the name, "Ethel," and beside the other, "Elsie."

Just as this card shows one example of sharing happiness, in the opening of gifts, may we not say that in a broader sense we were receiving gifts every day? God was sending us gifts, things that we at first did not recognize as gifts. What kind of gifts? I'll mention only a few—a pretty sunrise, the meadow lark singing, the flash of blue wings as the blue jay flew past our window, or the little chickadee that we saw perched on and looking into an empty glass milk bottle on our porch waiting for the milkman to pick it up. Yes, these things and many more, such as a neighbor stopping by to say "hello," showed us God's love. Indeed, almost every day was like Christmas for us.

Just as we felt like Alice in Wonderland going through the halls in the Village that first day here, so all our lives as we traveled together from place to place, sharing new experiences and pointing out marvelous things to each other, we found many treasures to store in our memory chests. Sharing made the treasures more meaningful.

Not All a "Bed of Roses"

Besides the fire there were a few other disturbing events to make us feel like being initiated. For one thing, on account of the fire the big back door, just a few yards away from us was left propped open day and night. Day wasn't so bad, although a few bees got in, but night was bad. We had heard about the black bear that had been seen near our part of the complex and we had seen the officers looking for him.

One dark night, we heard a pack of dogs barking and running past our end of the building. I said to Elsie, "I wonder if they are chasing that black bear?" So we checked again to see that we had our door well barricaded with furniture.

Then there was the mystery of the bluish light down on the rug on the floor in the hall. I called Elsie and she put her hand right down on it but didn't get burned, so we guessed it wasn't a "short" or electric wire burning. The next night we saw it again and as soon as morning came we called for the maintenance man. The third night the blue light was in the bathroom circling over the tub. I got brave, batted it down quickly with my faithful yardstick, and got it in a paper napkin. When the maintenance man came that morning we had saved exhibit "A" for him. He laughed, "That's a lightning bug!"

Elsie said, "What kind of lightning bugs do you grow down here in North Carolina? That's the biggest one I ever saw."

Here's another example of good luck. The first day we were in Hendersonville, after our arrival the night before, my sister was standing at the counter in the Village office. She remarked, "I wonder where there is a good bank." A man standing nearby told her a name and directed her how to get there. After some difficulty in finding it and then finding a parking place, we went into the lobby. I found a bench and Elsie went into a little enclosure nearby where she opened our new accounts. After putting our signatures on all the papers, Elsie tried to help me (with my artificial knee) up off that bench. A most gracious lady, the one who waited on Elsie, came out of her enclosure and practically lifted me to my feet. She said, "Let me be your personal banker. Just call me Dot." Mrs. Marlowe has been our special good friend ever since and has helped us so much in so many ways. We were certainly "greenhorns" when it came to financial affairs.

Another incident that same morning might qualify as a miniserendipity. In trying to locate the bank, I found myself driving out of town, so I looked for a place to turn. Good luck! There was the Buick showroom and garage on the right with the service door up. Since I had had so much experience with Buick places I dived right in and felt right at home. A pleasant man in a white coat was standing by the door and he gave me directions, including a good place to get turned. After thanking him, I asked if he was the service manager, and he said, "No, I am the owner."

That was boner No. 1. Then I remarked "I bought my Buick seven years ago and like it so well I'll never trade it in." Boner No. 2. However I did add, I always take it to Buick Service."

Elsie told me later, "You spoiled his prospect of ever selling you a new car."

Choosing a Doctor

One of the first requirements for new residents in Carolina Village was to record the name of your doctor in the office. Therefore, we called several doctors with the same response from all their receptionists, "Call again next month. We have an influx of Floridians up for the summer right now."

So we waited until July and succeeded in getting an appointment with Dr. Paul E. Hill. When we got home we compared notes as usual. Out of a clear sky the doctor had asked Elsie how we happened to come to him. Now, Elsie, quicker than I am, was ready with an answer, "Well, our doctor in Charleston was Dr. Hills, so we liked the name. Then we drove around your block and saw that you had a parking lot that my sister could get in." As an afterthought, she added, "of course, we heard people talking about you over at the Village." He could draw his own conclusions. You may have a different way to choose a doctor, but I must say we did all right.

Highlights of Living in the Village

In a previous chapter we mentioned evidences of our residents' artistic talent as we went through the halls of Carolina Village, but we did not tell about other talents. We are fortunate in having musicians of unusual talent who give us concerts regularly in our Village Hall.

Besides our own residents, we often have outside artists or speakers, sometimes a relative of a resident. I am thinking of Phyllis Wells, a well-known singer on television in Wales, who came often to see her parents here, and when she did we were sure to have a concert. She was so generous in giving her time and talent.

Residents who have hobbies, such as woodcarving, needlework, etc. have a chance to work on them in our craft rooms. Once a year we have an arts and crafts show. My sister and I usually put some of the rocks that we had polished and set on display.

There is no need to get lonesome for want of something to do. Other residents are interested in gardens, both vegetable and flower. For us, who had lived in International House, it reminded us of the variety of interests and talents there to be shared by all like one big happy family.

All in all, we enjoyed an ideal situation, and my sister was very happy here. If we do have a complaint (we seldom do), we just go to see "Doley." Everyone calls him that. Doley is

Mr. Doley Bell, our administrator, a big man with big shoulders and a big heart.

Good Fortune Again

A month after we had arrived and were fairly well settled in our new home in Carolina Village we started talking about transferring our membership in Alpha Delta Kappa to a local chapter. We hunted up a copy of the *Kappan* and found the name and officers of the Alpha Upsilon Chapter here in Henderson County.

That's as far as we got. We had not written any letters of inquiry or made any telephone calls about it yet, but that same day we opened up the evening paper and saw a picture of the newly elected state president, Mary Ruth Heil, and the new state corresponding secretary, Florence Wallace. They were going to the regional meeting of our sorority in Nashville, Tennessee, the next week. The newly elected officers of the local chapter, Alpha Upsilon, were also listed. We were delighted. What good luck! No need to write letters now.

Elsie called Mary Ruth, and she called Florence. They both came to our apartment, bringing us a potted African violet, our sorority flower. It is still living, a memorial of their friendliness to a "sister." If I'm in need, some of the sisters are right here. When either of us was in the hospital or ill at home, flowers and cards always arrived. We were able to act as hostesses at the Village for several of their meetings and gave a program one time for them.

At the memorial for Elsie in our Village Hall twenty of my "sisters" came even though it was a busy Saturday afternoon. Florence and some of the other sisters come regularly to visit me and help me. Yes, that chance noticing of the picture in the paper led to untold pleasure and satisfaction in finding a chapter of congenial, friendly sorority sisters. That meant so much to us, for our only relatives are three cousins living in California—too far away for us to see very often.

One highlight of our being members of our local chapter was the opportunity to go to the Governor's summer mansion in Asheville in October 1981 to a reception in honor of Mary Ruth. One of our sisters, Dot Meador, took us, for we would never have found the place, located high up on a hill overlooking the whole valley.

It was a festive occasion and we met many of the North Carolina girls, including one who had lived in Charleston and had been in Kansas City when we were there. On the way home, Dot took us for a ride on the Blue Ridge Parkway to see the beautiful fall colors. They were gorgeous and helped to make this a day to be remembered.

Rockhounds Meet

One of the activities that we enjoyed very much after coming to Carolina Village was going to the meeting of the Gem and Mineral Society each month, where we met other rockhounds. There were usually forty members present, who shared their experiences and brought samples of what they had found to put on the exhibit table.

Fortunately there were two other residents, Mr. and Mrs. Roderick Randel, who attended these meetings, and they took us in their car. When we gave a program for the group, we were able to buy a few slides from *Arizona Highways* magazine to add to our own. These slides, being professional work, were clearer and more colorful than ours. For example, when we showed scenes in the Petrified Forest, you should have heard the "Oh's" and "Ah's," as those beautiful stumps, entirely turned to agate showed every color of the rainbow.

In this club, we had a small part in getting young people interested in rocks and minerals. After all, North Carolina is known as a "rockhound's paradise." The club offers a scholarship each year to a college student.

At their annual gem and mineral show we can learn more about our hobby and buy specimens for our collections. One of the biggest thrills I had was having an appraiser tell me, "Yes, that is a piece of yellow jade!"

I had found it at Patrick's Point, California, and even the jeweler who polished one side of it, the side with the black "fern" dendritics on it, did not know what it was. Recently I read in a *Gem and Minerals* magazine that dendritic jade is rare but has been found in California. Also in a book on jade that I bought I found a whole paragraph describing the beach at

Patrick's Point and stating that the rare black jade had been fond there. The name for it is chloromelanite (from the Greek for "green" and for "black"). Word derivations are really fascinating.

In 1953 on that same beach I found a lens-shaped piece of dark green jade, which I had polished and put on a necklace. The next day when I went into a little restaurant at the head of the trail, the waitress said, "You know, there was a girl on the beach here yesterday who found a piece of jade!" I didn't say I was the one.

My sister and I were very happy to find some of these beauties of nature and to share them with others. We were thrilled also to find several "water" agates, but not knowing that rocks were porous, we failed to keep them moist and the water evaporated after several years. We don't have many fossils, but those we have are interesting. There is one, a gastropod, where the middle spiral part has turned to translucent agate. Truly nature is full of wonderful things.

Thinking of Elsie, it made me very happy to put an exhibit of our rocks and minerals in the glass showcase in the Carolina Village lounge. She had done most of the polishing and mounting in sets. I felt that I was doing it as a memorial to her. On the title card I printed: "Bits of Beauty from God's Creation." We both agreed that these marvelous things in nature had to have a divine Creator and we had so expressed it in the introduction to all our slide programs on our hobby.

History Repeats Itself

We have often heard it said that history repeats itself. That was true for us in 1982, for we had both been in the hospital at the same time in 1977. So it was in 1982. In Pardee Hospital I had both hip joints and one knee joint renewed.

Elsie had a lump on her upper chest biopsied, and the report came back "cancer returned." The very day that I came home to the Med Center, she went to Asheville for her first chemotherapy treatment. Our good friend here, Ruth Aleshire, took her and looked after her so faithfully that year.

A year later, when Elsie went for other tests, Florence and her friend took us. The fall colors were gorgeous on all the surrounding hills. We were inspired by the beauty around us and thought about God's goodness to us all. We were truly thankful. The next day, another gorgeous one, Elsie went back for chest X-rays and this times Eula Studebaker, a friend in the Village, took us.

Those reports were all good, but a year later Elsie had to have surgery again, and we rejoiced because it was successful. However, only six months later the cancer had spread to the liver. A friend and I went with her to Asheville for chemotherapy. In December she went into the hospital, just as she had prophesied in June, when she said to me in a calm voice, "It will be around Christmas time."

In the two intervening years, 1983 and 1984, she had been as active as usual. We gave slide programs on our hobby for the Village residents and for Gem and Mineral Society. We had previously given a similar one for our sorority. In July 1984 Elsie gave a talk on jasper for the Gem and Mineral group. This talk, which was five minutes long, was her "penalty" for having won the door prize, a piece of red jasper, the month before. In the meantime she had sawed a piece off it, polished it, and mounted it on a necklace to show the group. I had memorized her speech and had reassured her that I would give it for her if she couldn't give it.

Wonderful Friends

When we moved into Carolina Village it was our good fortune to have as neighbors across the hall Mr. and Mrs. Oliphant. She not only told us about the fire but explained many things, such as the ring system, whereby we let the ring checkers know if we are all right simply by having our ring on our doorknob by 9:00 every evening and taken in by 9:00 every morning.

You can't go into Pardee Hospital at any entrance without seeing a big metal plaque naming Virginia and Milo Oliphant as the donors of the equipment or other facility in that wing for the benefit of the patients. I was in twice and my sister twice, so we benefited by their generosity, especially on the surgical floor.

If we had not moved into the apartment across the hall from

them, we might never have met Norma Hyder, a licensed practical nurse, who took care of them in the daytime. Now that Mr. Oliphant has died, she still comes to care for Mrs. Oliphant on the first shift and supervises getting nurses for the other shifts.

Norma is a wonderful, Christian friend to eveyone. She has been my constant adviser and helper. When Elsie was in the hospital the first time, Normal came a few minutes early so that she could help me get dressed to go to see her. (Elsie used to call me on the phone around 5:00 A.M. to see if I had set the alarm for 5:30.)

When Elsie was in the hospital last year, Norma came to get me every morning and then came for me in the evening. Going back to the days when Elsie went to Asheville for chemotherapy twice a month. Norma took us, and when she couldn't our good sorority sister, Ellen Sharpe, did.

I can't begin to enumerate all the good things Norma has done for me and is doing. She took me to Elsie's memorial service and regularly takes me to the store. She watches my supplies of food and medicines. In short, she just looks out for me like one of her family.

Not a day goes by that I don't think how fortunate I am to live here, where I not only have Norma but other friends, whose sole purpose in life is to help others.

How Many Ethel Joneses?

I have often wondered how many Ethel Joneses there are around. Perhaps some of the mail I receive is meant for someone else with my name. My sister got telephone calls frequently after we moved here for some other Elsie Jones.

Once while we were still in Charleston, I received a letter requesting the use of our house for headquarters for a Republican candidate for President in the upcoming primary. I couldn't accommodate them. We lived in an apartment and I was getting ready for knee surgery. Anyhow it must have been a mistake, for I had never contributed enough to warrant such a request. It may be that the Republicans were "few and far between" that year in West Virginia.

Four years later, after we had moved here I was invited to

sit on the platform at the national convention. I know that was wrong, for my twin sister did not receive an invitation. She got an invitation to attend a reception at International House in Berkeley to celebrate their fiftieth anniversary, but I didn't. Did someone think there was only one of us?

When it came to writing I could not get my sister to show any of her "stories" to anyone but to me. She always was afraid they weren't good enough. I had a principal who pushed me, although he did not lighten my schedule to give me time for writing.

One of my latest stories he sent to the editor of our state education journal. She wrote him a note of thanks in accepting it, but she died that summer, and my story evidently died in the hands of the new editors. They changed the format entirely from a magazine on glossy paper to a news bulletin on regular newsprint.

A story that had been published before the changeover was "Those Rating Sheets," and the very next month my name was on the cover in big print, "Sympathy for Ethel." People would wonder who Ethel was.

The letter that started all this speculation about "how many Ethel Joneses," came just this winter inviting me to go on a cruise to Antarctica to follow the course of Magellan and Drake. I like the pictures in the brochure of penguins all massed together on the beach like a convention crowd waiting for their ship to dock.

I laughed to myself as I pictured my wheelchair bobbing around over that terrain at the South Pole. The envelope on the outside had "The pleasure of your company is requested." I could hardly wait to open it to see what kind of invitation it was. I'm really sorry I couldn't go, but I will enjoy the story and pictures when they appear in that magazine. I have received other brochures since then and I know what to expect. I am studying their maps and learning some geography, which is always changing. It's good to keep at least your mind active.

I used to grumble because we were just numbers. I wanted my name used, but now perhaps it's a good thing after all to be known by our Social Security number or some other I.D. to avoid confusion and to make it safer for us.

Once I remember, when we were on one of our train trips

and had time to spare in the Union Station in Chicago, Elsie and I looked up our names in the telephone book. There were five Ethel Joneses and five Elsie Joneses. The first year I taught I had an Ethel Jones in class, and Elsie saw an "Elsie Jones" on the staff of their school paper for the previous year. Mother's name was Ethel, and we had an Ethel Jones cooking in one of our schools. Another Ethel Jones got one of my checks by mistake and sent it to me. So that year Charleston tied with Chicago on my name.

This year about a week after my sister's obituary had been in the paper, I picked my paper up one morning and saw "Ethel M. Jones" in the obituary column. I knew it didn't refer to me. I knew about this woman, for I had received a piece of her mail once. Some of my friends were a little startled.

Perhaps the statisticians can figure out how many other people have my name. The most amazing coincidence was narrated in a news story that we saw in a newspaper in Kansas City when we were there for our sorority convention in 1969. There was a picture of Ethel Jones, a Latin teacher in some city in India; she was getting ready to take a plane for Europe, as a retirement gift from her pupils.

The analogy stops with her being a teacher of Latin and retiring that year, because I did not receive a trip abroad, although I did teach Latin and had retired in 1969. The truth is stranger than fiction sometimes.

There wasn't much chance of confusion over Father's name for I doubt if there was ever anyone else with his full name— Cyrus Leander Jones. Mother always called him Lee, and usually on addresses he was listed with just initials—C.L. When we were little, Elsie used to tell her playmates that her initials were L.C.—just the reverse of Father's.

Spiritual Food

All during the summer and fall of 1985, when my sister was taking strong doses of chemotherapy, she never complained of being hungry, although she would not eat much on account of her sore mouth. On Sundays when we had a buffet at noon, I brought her tray to her, but she was more interested in telling me all about the sermon she had just heard on the television while I was gone. I was really happy to hear her giving thanks for her food and all her blessings, because I knew that her mind was overcoming the pain by thinking of Him, the source of all good things.

When she was in the hospital, it was the same. She talked and joked with her nurses in trying, I'm sure, to get her mind off herself. About the only time she mentioned herself was to lament that she had not done more in an evangelistic way. She wished that we had been more active in the church by teaching Sunday School. I reminded her that she had been a school teacher and that her influence was greater than she realized. She had set an example.

When I observed her nurses, I was thankful that God put it into the hearts of some people to be doctors or nurses. They have a sense of humor too and can cheer a patient up. One nurse that came on at 7:00 A.M. used to say with delight to the other nurses as they came in, "I have two patients," and look over at me sitting in a wheelchair. Then she would add, "The one in the chair is more trouble than this one in bed," and Elsie was amused.

The day I wore the locket which Elsie had made, with our pictures in it, she noticed it immediately as soon as I entered and said, "Oh, you wore our locket!"

I let the nurses see it and three out of four of them pointed to my picture and said, "That's Elsie!" She was pleased over that, for she was losing her hair.

There was just one time when the morphine made her go out of her head. That was one evening when she had three visitors. She told each one she was "Ethel Jones" and rattled the side rails on her bed. The nurses had told me, but I didn't say a word. She herself spoke up and told me later she had thought they were coming to take her to the morgue because she saw them putting a sign on her door "Deceased" and she did not want to be buried when she was still alive. So she told them my name, and she shook the bedrails to let them know she was still living. She was up to her old "twin tricks" even then.

Bears (or representations of bears) have come into our lives on several occasions. The first, naturally, was with teddy bears, when we were two years old. Our teddy bears, which we had thrown and batted around, suddenly disappeared. Mother said they had left because they were being mistreated. Then one day we heard a knock, and Mother said, "Let's see who is at the door."

We went and there were our teddy bears, dressed in new outfits standing on the porch. (I don't know how Mother ever got them to stand.) Immediately we had them in our arms loving them, and we took good care of them after that.

Years later, when we were in Yellowstone National Park, we saw real bears. Elsie asked the fellow who showed us to our cabin what to do if we saw a bear. He replied, "Pick up a rock and throw at it." With that he stooped and got one out of the driveway and handed it to her.

She put it in her purse, and after we came home, she put it in a box with some of our "precious" stones that we had collected. I still have it labeled "Elsie's bear rock." People, wondered, suppose, what that ordinary-looking rock is doing in there with those agates and jaspers.

On Christmas Day last year (1985) Norma Hyder had seen to it that there were two huge Christmas stockings hanging in Elsie's hospital room. Peeking out of the top of each stocking was a soft, little, cuddly, brown teddy bear. Elsie handled hers so carefully and had it placed, so that she could see it all the time.

Norma's thoughtfulness helped to make our day a happy one. Other people helped to "make our day" too, but I can't recount it all here. Florence, who had been with us every day like a real "sister," put up decorations and brought our dinner up from the cafeteria so that we could eat with Elsie in her room. Being a member of a church choir, she sang Christmas carols for us from a book I had brought. It was a very gratifying day for all of us, including the nurses.

Just one year before that memorable trip in 1965 when we had heard the hymn, "God Will Take Care of You," as we were driving through storms in Arizona, as previously related, Mother had asked us, "How will you girls get along?" Lying there in her hospital bed, she had evidently been worrying about us.

Elsie was quick to answer reassuring her, "God will take care of us." He did, not only during those storms, but all the time.

This year, when Elsie was in the hospital, she remarked to Norma that she was wondering who would take care of me. Norma reassured her by saying, "I'll take care of Ethel," and Elsie nestled back on her pillows satisfied.

She told me about it afterward with such a feeling of contentment. Norma has done so much for me and still is, as God directs her, for He has put it into her heart to help others. I am one of the fortunate recipients of that love.

Living Memorials

Last winter I was overjoyed when I received word that a tree had been planted as a living memorial to Elsie in one of our national forests. I cherish this sentence from the letter to me: "We know you share with us the hope that this tree will grow in full measure to bring beauty to the landscape and pleasure to all who pass its way."

Elsie had given the title "Beauty from the Earth" to her part of our slide programs and in it she said that one of our favorite hymns was "For the Beauty of the Earth."

When I received word from the Christian Broadcasting Network that a "living memorial" had been made in her name, I realized that this memorial would be "living" in the sense that lives of people would be changed in their being helped to come to a knowledge of Christ, bringing them both joy and peace. These memorials are better than stone monuments.

Our North Carolina Alpha Delta Kappa Sorority. Fidelis Nu chapter, is setting up a scholarship fund in Elsie's name. I will be so happy knowing that her ideals will be perpetuated in giving some deserving young person an opportunity for a college education. There is no better way to memorialize a teacher than to stress scholarship by providing funds for it.

Recently I read in a Charleston paper that the appropriations Committee in the U.S. Senate had recommended the expenditure of $8,000,000 for scholarships in West Virginia in the name of Senator Robert C. Byrd, who had served our state so well. I say "our" state because my sister and I lived there from 1910 to 1980, when we moved to North Carolina.

I wrote to Senator Byrd to congratulate him and received such a nice reply. In it he mentions my "taking time to write as I did." My stars! I should have apologized to him for his having to take time, busy as he is with world affairs, to read my handwritten note. I really did feel embarrassed to think about it after I had sent it, but the impulse was so strong. I am proud of our state and of Senator Byrd.

Yes, I am like my father. I do things on impulse, like writing letters.

Since I wrote the paragraphs above, I have read about a Yeager Scholarship program sponsored by Marshall University in Huntington, West Virginia. Named for "Chuck" Yeager, a native West Virginian, it will select outstanding high school seniors in the nation to be honored with a scholarship each year. It too will cost around $8 million part of which has already been collected, mostly through individual contributions to the Foundation Funds.

Dark Days

Mother often quoted, "Into each life some rain must fall." Dark days for us were in 1931, when Father died suddenly from a heart attack; again in 1964 when Mother passed away after a long illness, and for me, the most recent was in January this year when my dear twin sister was taken.

I do feel her presence all around me, and I know that her spirit still lives. That gives me joy and the courage to do what I think she would approve. I took pleasure in handlng the rocks she had polished, getting them ready for an exhibit in our Carolina lounge.

Like Mother she often quoted from Whittier's hymns and

from "Snow-Bound." Two lines all three of us treasured are:
        "Life is ever Lord of Death,
        And Love can never lose its own."
Another poem we like was Longfellow's "A Psalm of Life,"
especially the lines:
        "Dust thou art, to dust returneth
        Was not spoken of the soul."
Just recently I found among my souvenirs in a purse a little poem by Margaret Widdener called "The Watcher." I had carried it ever since Mother left us in 1964. In the poem the mother is described as always watching for the children to come home, and in the last stanza she is "watching from Heaven's window."

Also with these treasures is a paragraph that Florence Wallace wrote for inclusion in the newsletter for our sorority. This is it.

"Elsie Mabel Jones entered Omega Chapter January 2, 1986. She was a jewel that God polished by faith. Humility and courage were two of the facets cut by adversity into her character, but they only increased her brilliance. We of North Carolina Alpha Upsilon who have had her as a friend and sister will, if we follow her example, be better Alpha Delta Kappas and better Christians." I treasure this tribute more than I can express. It has helped me immensely.

Meet the Twins

When we attended our first Sunday night supper at Internations House, we were surprised and pleased to have people coming up to us saying, "We heard you were here, and we wanted to meet the twins."

Now there wasn't anything unsual about us except that we were twins and people could not tell us apart. Most of our lives we weighed exactly the same and had our hair combed alike. We dressed alike through W.V.U. days. If we did not, we heard comments, "What's the matter? Did you disagree this morning?"

To tell the truth, we always liked the same things. I remember a milliner who had to make a copy of a certain hat because she only had one, and we both wanted it. An optician had to order frames for Elsie just like mine, because she didn't see any others she liked.

One time after we were teaching and no longer dressed alike, we got a dress with buttons down the front, making it easier when we had a doctor's appointment. We called it our "doctor" dress. One morning Elsie wore it to the doctor, and as I had an appointment with him in the afternoon. I wore it, causing some confusion, for the receptionist said, "We don't want you; we want your sister. We had you this morning."

I had to convince her that I was just wearing the same dress that my sister had worn earlier.

Now, dear unknown readers, you have "met the twins," and I hope you were pleased with the introduction and could live vicariously for a time at least the life of a twin. I've heard many people say, "I wish I were a twin." We were happy indeed that we were twins and shared so many joys.

Journey's End

Somehow two lines from Stevenson's "Requiem" keep running through my mind,

> "Home is the sailor, home from the sea,
> And the hunter home from the hill."

I like the musical lilt and the alliteration of the lines as well as the thought. They inspired me to write these lines about my dear twin sister. Although they don't have the lilt and the alliteration of a great writer like Stevenson, they do express my feeling about my sister:

> Home is my sister, in the Presence of God,
> Leaving her prints in the pathways she's trod.
> No, my dear sister isn't under the sod,
> She is waiting for you and for me.

> This is the end of my story true.
> Hoping that it has been pleasing to you.
> Now I must say a belated adieu
> Knowing my twin's forever free.

In her letter of condolence to me, Eugenia Price expressed it in words very appropriate for school teachers, when she said that Elsie would be waiting for us, "when we graduate from Earth's schoolroom."